SIMPLY SCRUMPTIOUS MICROWAVING

Mary Ann Feuchter Robinson
Rosemary Dunn Stancil
Lorela Nichols Wilkins

David & Charles
Newton Abbot   London

Dedicated to our husbands and children
for their patience and encouragement
during the writing of this book

Anglicisation of American text: Margaret Weale

British Library Cataloguing in Publication Data

Robinson, Mary Ann Feuchter
Simply scrumptious microwaving.
1. Microwave cookery
I. Title   II. Stancil, Rosemary Dunn
III. Wilkins, Lorela Nichols
641.5'882   TX832

ISBN 0-7153-8798-7 (hardback)
ISBN 0-7153-8878-9 (paperback)

First published in the United States of America in 1982
by Simply Scrumptious Inc

Phototypeset by Typesetters (Birmingham) Ltd
Smethwick, West Midlands
and printed in Great Britain
by Redwood Burn Ltd, Trowbridge, Wilts
for David & Charles Publishers plc
Brunel House   Newton Abbot   Devon

Contents

Introduction to Simply Scrumptious Microwaving

The microwave oven is a unique cooking appliance that is becoming an indispensable piece of equipment in the kitchen. It is not intended to replace the conventional cooker. However, with experience you may easily find yourself using it for 80% to 90% of your cooking. Results achieved with the microwave oven depend on the cook who operates the oven. Remember, you control the microwave oven and the food that is prepared. As with conventional cooking, do not be afraid to experiment and learn to use the microwave in your own style, utilising your skills, talents and creativity.

For good results, it is necessary to learn recommended techniques for determining cooking times of various foods and to make judgements as the food cooks. Also, it is very important that you be familiar with the instruction manual that came with your microwave.

The authors of this book have converted numerous 'old favourite' recipes to microwaving. Many recipes in this book provide a guide for food preparation with a back-to-basics approach, emphasizing the natural goodness and ease of 'scratch' cooking in the microwave. For example, you will find many recipes using fresh vegetables and fruits, giving a straight-from-the-garden taste – with little seasoning necessary. All recipes used in *Simply Scrumptious Microwaving* have been tested and developed for accuracy by professional home economists, making this a book that will please and delight you for years to come.

Timing Adjustments: All recipes have been developed and tested using 600 to 700 watt microwave units. Know what your microwave oven's wattage is and make adjustments accordingly, using this chart.

400 to 500 watt unit: Add 30 seconds to each minute for cooking time.

500 to 600 watt unit: Add 15 seconds to each minute of cooking time.

Cook the shortest amount of time that is recommended and add more time if necessary. After preparing recipes in this book you may find it convenient to note the times and power settings which work best in your oven.

Power Setting: Recipes in this book are designed to be used with all types of microwave ovens. The term HIGH means full or 100% power. Reduced power levels such as 80%, 70%, 50%, 30% or 10% are used because different manufacturers assign different names to levels of power. Check your instruction manual or oven cookbook to find settings on your oven that correspond to the percentage settings found in this book.

Utensils: Begin with what you have. Many 'microwave utensils' are already in your kitchen even though you may have never considered using them for cooking.

Glass: Most types of glass may be used for heating. For primary cooking, use only *HEAT TEMPERED GLASS*. Heat from the food will break glass that is not heat tempered. Glass measuring cups make excellent utensils.

Paper: Paper products are an excellent choice for heating foods and as coverings to absorb moisture and splattering during cooking. Paper cups, plates, napkins, towels and greaseproof paper are examples.

Plastic Roasting bags: To use, lay the pouch in a dish to catch drips and make steam vents by piercing the top of the bag.

China, Stoneware, Pottery and Porcelain: Most dinnerware is suitable for heating foods. Some dinnerware, however, does contain materials that will absorb microwave energy and cause the dish to become hot and possibly break. If in doubt, test the dish. To test, measure 100–200ml (4–8fl oz) water in a cup. Place the cup of water and dish in the oven. Water cup can be placed in or on the dish. Microwave on HIGH 1–2 minutes. If the dish remains cool, it is suitable for microwaving. If the dish feels hot, it is not suitable for microwaving because it could become too hot during cooking and break. Never use a dish with metal trim, for example, a gold trim. The metallic trim may discolour and the dish could break.

Wood, Straw and Seashells: Wood and other natural materials are suitable if the cooking time is very short. For example, warming a basket of bread rolls for 1 minute. Wood has a tendency to absorb moisture and fats which cause it to heat up, dry out, and ultimately split if exposed to long periods of cooking.

Metal: Metal should not be used as a primary cooking utensil because microwaves cannot pass through metal. Some microwave ovens allow limited use of metal. Examples are aluminium foil for shielding, frozen convenience dinner trays with sides that measure less than 1.8cm (¾in) and metal skewers filled with food. (Be sure to check your oven manufacturer's instruction manual.)

Dish Shape: Foods cook more evenly in round dishes than square or rectangular-shaped ones. If you cook in square-shaped dishes, shielding the corners is often advised to prevent overcooking. Ring moulds are excellent for foods that do not need to be stirred during microwaving, because energy penetrates food from the centre, sides, top and bottom for more even cooking.

Arrangement: It is important to minimise differences in shape and density of food in order to assure uniform cooking. Place less dense or thinner areas towards the centre of the dish, with more dense and thicker areas to the outside. Examples might be:

When cooking several potatoes, place smaller ones to the centre.
When cooking chicken legs, place meaty parts to the outside of the dish.
Place broccoli florets in the centre with tougher stems to the outside. Rearrange foods that cannot be stirred midway through cooking time to help foods cook more evenly.

Factors Determining Cooking Time:

Starting Temperature: It is necessary to make timing adjustments when using refrigerated or very warm ingredients. If a cold food is put in the microwave oven, the cooking time will be longer.

Volume: The larger the volume of food, the longer the cooking time. When doubling a recipe, increase the time by about ½ and check the food is cooked, adding extra time if necessary.

Density: Dense, heavy foods take longer to microwave than porous, airy ones. Food will also change in density, depending on the way it is prepared. Roast beef is denser than minced beef; mashed potatoes will not hold heat as long as a baked potato. Foods that have a high level of sugar or fat also cook quickly.

Stirring: Cooking time is shortened by stirring and rearranging, equalising the internal temperature by bringing the hotter outside areas to the cooler centre portion.

Covering: In microwaving, covering serves the same purpose as in conventional cooking. The cover holds in steam to tenderise food, keep it moist and shorten cooking time. A general rule is – if you would cover conventionally, cover during microwaving. When tight covers are needed such as when cooking rice, use clingfilm. Loose coverings like paper towels or greaseproof paper prevent splattering.

Moisture, Fat and Sugar: Cooking time is affected by the amount of moisture, fat and sugar present in the food being microwaved. Foods containing high fat and sugar levels heat very quickly and may reach higher temperatures than foods having low fat and sugar levels. Foods having lower fat and sugar levels require longer cooking time.

Extension Leads: The microwave oven should never be set up to operate on an extension lead.

Rotating: If your oven has an even cooking pattern, this procedure is not necessary. Follow your manufacturer's directions.

Shielding: The purpose of shielding is to slow down the cooking process, preventing less dense areas from overcooking. Use small pieces of foil (if permitted in your oven) to shield areas that may overcook. For example, shielding is usually necessary on chicken wings and drumsticks and large pieces of meat, where some sections may cook faster than desired.

Standing Time: To prevent overcooking, it is very important that you allow for standing time. Foods continue to cook by internal heat when removed from the oven. The cooking process will continue for 1–15 minutes depending on the size, shape and density of the food being cooked.

Converting Recipes: To convert a recipe for use in the microwave, find a similar microwave recipe and start with the same amount of the main ingredients. Reduce liquids by ¼ and use slightly less seasonings. Reduce conventional time by ¼ to ⅓.

Simply Scrumptious
Appetizers and Beverages

General Guidelines

It is possible for the hostess to join the party and relax by using the microwave! Follow the suggestions listed below for successful appetizers and beverages:

Remember that many appetizers have heat-sensitive ingredients such as cheese, sour cream, mayonnaise, eggs or meats that need to be cooked on a lower power setting. A setting between 50 to 70% power is usually recommended.

Select crackers for appetizers that are sturdy since the microwave does not dry food. Prepare appetizer fillings before the party, but do not place on crackers until just before ready to microwave or the base will become soggy.

Remember, it is possible to heat many appetizers in serving dishes in the microwave.

Cover appetizers only when a recipe specifies.

Take advantage of the convenience of heating many beverages on HIGH until just before the boiling point is reached for full flavour.

Shrimp Appetizer Tree
A beautiful party decoration at Christmas time!
Decorate tree with an assortment of raw vegetables
along with the shrimps to look very festive.

General directions for cooking shrimps:
Arrange shrimps in baking dish in a single layer and cook on HIGH power 3–5 minutes per 450g (1lb). Microwave for ½ the time and stir, bringing the shrimps on the outside to the centre. Microwave remaining time and when shrimps turn pink and opaque, remove from oven and let stand covered 1–2 minutes.

Directions for making tree:
Select a styrofoam cone and cover completely with parsley, endive, or mustard greens. Anchor greens on tree with floral wire picks and secure to tray by using coloured sellotape. Secure shrimps and vegetables to tree with coloured cocktail sticks.

Toasted Pecans or Peanuts

Place 225g (8oz) pecans or peanuts in a 22.5cm (9in) pie plate and microwave on HIGH for 5–6 minutes. Stir every 2 minutes. Add butter and salt at end of cooking time if desired. (Peanuts may take slightly longer to roast.)

Shrimply Scrumptious Spread
Quick and delicious served with crackers

225g (½lb) defrosted shrimps
1 can 295g (10.4oz) condensed
    cream of shrimp or crab bisque
    soup
225g (8oz) cream cheese
2 × 15ml tbsp (2tbsp) chopped

parsley or chives
1 × 5ml tsp (1tsp) garlic salt
1 × 5ml tsp (1tsp) horseradish
1 × 15ml tbsp (1tbsp) lemon juice
2 × 15ml tbsp (2tbsp) tomato
    ketchup

Place shrimps in a baking dish in a single layer and cover with clingfilm. Microwave on HIGH 1½–2½ minutes, stirring after cooking 1 minute. Cook until shrimp turns pink and opaque. Set aside. Soften cream cheese for 45 seconds to 1 minute on 70% power and combine with soup. Beat in electric mixer or food processor until smooth. Add shrimp, parsley, garlic salt, horseradish, lemon juice and ketchup. Stir until mixed.

Scrumptious Crab Dip
Quick and elegant

325g (12oz) crabmeat
325g (12oz) mature Cheddar
  cheese, grated
225g (8oz) Cheshire cheese, grated

50ml (2fl oz) single cream
100ml (4fl oz) dry white wine
1 × 2.5ml tsp (½tsp) white pepper
2 garlic cloves, crushed

Place cream in a 2 litre (3½pt) casserole. Microwave on 50% power 2–3 minutes until hot, but not boiling. Add cheeses and garlic, stirring to blend. Microwave for 4–6 minutes at 50%, stirring vigorously every 2 minutes with a wire whip or fork. Add crabmeat, wine and pepper and cook 2 additonal minutes. Transfer to a chafing dish or fondue pot set on low heat. Serve with croûtons or sesame sticks.

Spicy Pups

1 jar 250g (10oz) redcurrant jelly
4 × 15ml tbsp (4tbsp) prepared
  mustard

450g (1lb) frankfurters

Place jelly and mustard in 1.5 litre (2½pt) glass casserole. Beat well with wire whisk or rotary beater as mustard is added and microwave on 70% power 3–5 minutes. Cut frankfurters crosswise into bite size pieces. Add to jelly and mustard mixture and cook for 3–5 minutes on HIGH until frankfurters are hot. Place in chafing dish and serve with cocktail sticks.

Basic Cream Cheese Spread

225g (8oz) cream cheese
Grated onion
1 × 1.25ml tsp (¼tsp) salt

1 × 1.25ml tsp (¼tsp) white
  pepper

10

Soften cream cheese in microwave 1–1½ minutes on 70% power. Add onion, salt and white pepper along with your favourite variation listed below.

Cucumber sandwiches: Grate 5cm (2in) cucumber and add cream cheese mixture, stirring to blend.

Shrimp spread: Add 100g (4oz) deveined shrimp to cream cheese mixture adding sour cream or milk until right consistency is reached.

Cream cheese and pimento spread: Add pimento and 2 × 5ml tsp (2tsp) dry sherry, stirring to blend.

Spring onion and cream cheese: Add finely chopped spring onion instead of grated onion to basic cream cheese spread.

Pineapple spread: Add pineapple jam and chopped nuts to 225g (8oz) cream cheese and stir to blend.

Party Sandwiches

225g (8oz) cream cheese
2 × 15ml tbsp (2tbsp) finely chopped green pepper
2 × 15ml tbsp (2tbsp) grated onion
3 × 15ml tbsp (3tbsp) pimento

3 hard-boiled eggs, finely chopped
150g (6oz) finely chopped pecans or walnuts
1 × 5ml tsp (1tsp) salt
2.5ml tsp (½tsp) white pepper

Soften cream cheese for 2 minutes on 50% power. Stir in remaining ingredients and microwave for 2–3 additional minutes to blend flavours.

Sandwich Fan

Make an interesting sandwich display by cutting a paper pattern in a fan shape. Cut bread shapes from the pattern and use varying colours and fillings on each row. Garnish with cheese, chives, olives and spring onions, etc.

Sweet and Celery Nuts

25g (1oz) butter
150g (6oz) peanuts
100g (4oz) walnut halves

1 × 5ml tsp (1tsp) celery salt
150g (6oz) raisins

Microwave butter for 30–40 seconds. Add nuts and celery salt, stirring until nuts are coated with butter. Cook on HIGH for 6 minutes, stirring every 2 minutes. Add raisins. Serve warm.

Saucy Crab Ball
Makes a nice showing with crab piled on top

450g (1lb) crabmeat
450g (1lb) cream cheese, softened
1 small onion, finely chopped
1 × 5ml tsp (1tsp) lemon juice

4 × 15ml tbsp (4tbsp) seafood
   sauce
Garlic powder to taste
Worcestershire sauce to taste

Microwave cream cheese for 1–2 minutes on 50% power. Add everything except crabmeat and seafood sauce. Form a ball. Pile crab over top of ball and top with seafood sauce. Serve with bite size pastry shells, toasted fingers or bland biscuits.

Braunschweiger

450g (1lb) braunschweiger (liver-
   wurst or liver sausage)
1 × 2.5ml tsp (½tsp) garlic
   powder

1 × 2.5ml tsp (½tsp) basil
3 × 15ml tbsp (3tbsp) finely
   chopped onions

Coating:
225g (8oz) cream cheese
A few drops Tabasco

1 × 5ml tsp (1tsp) mayonnaise
Garlic powder to taste

Soften braunschweiger for 20 seconds on HIGH and then add garlic powder, basil and onions. Shape into ball or mound. To make coating, soften cream cheese 45 seconds to 1 minute on HIGH. Add Tabasco, mayonnaise and add garlic powder to taste. Ice the braunschweiger with the cream cheese mixture. Garnish and serve with toast.

Garnish with black olives, dill or parsley sprigs.
Use canapé cutters to cut sliced cheese into desired shapes.

Quick Pizza Fondue
Children love this dish!

Serves 6

1 × 22g (4/5oz) pkt cheese sauce
2 × 15ml tbsp (2tbsp) tomato
  ketchup
1 × 2.5ml tsp (½tsp) oregano

Dash of garlic powder or a crushed
  garlic clove
100g (4oz) mature Cheddar cheese

Prepare cheese sauce. Stir and add remaining ingredients. Microwave for 1–2 minutes on 50% power. Serve with bite size pieces of French bread, apples, celery or green pepper.

Beef Dip
Quick, easy and spicy!

225g (8oz) cream cheese
65g (2½oz) cooked beef (chopped
  finely)
2 × 15ml tbsp (2tbsp) chopped

onion
2 × 15ml tbsp (2tbsp) milk
50ml (2fl oz) sour cream
1 × 2.5ml tsp (½tsp) black pepper

Soften cheese in microwave for 1–2 minutes on 70% power. Mix other ingredients together with cheese and microwave 3–4 minutes on 70% power stirring halfway through cooking time.

Artichoke Pan Quiche
Scrumptious as a hot appetizer

Serves 6–8 (per Quiche)

4 × 15ml tbsp (4tbsp) onion,
  chopped
1 garlic clove, crushed
4 eggs
1 × 400g (14oz) can artichoke
  hearts, drained and chopped

25g (1oz) breadcrumbs
225g (½lb) cheese, grated
2 × 15ml tbsp (2tbsp) chopped
  parsley
1 × 2.5ml tsp (½tsp) each of
  oregano, salt and Tabasco

13

Microwave onion and garlic clove for 1–2 minutes on HIGH. Beat eggs and add remaining ingredients. Place mixture in two 20cm (8in) square dishes. (Freeze one for later if desired.) Shield corners with foil if oven permits use of metal. Microwave 10–12 minutes at 70% power. Let stand 5 minutes before serving.

Ham Cheese Rolls
Prepare in advance and freeze.
Great to serve at a buffet or luncheon.

60 servings

450g (1lb) minced ham
225g (8oz) butter at room temperature
3 × 15ml tbsp (3tbsp) poppy seeds
1 × 5ml tsp (1tsp) Worcestershire sauce

3 × 15ml tbsp (3tbsp) mustard
1 medium onion, grated
325g (¾lb) cheese, grated
60 small party rolls or 30 finger buffet rolls, halved

Mix all ingredients except rolls. Slice rolls and fill with mixture. To serve, place rolls on paper-towel-lined plate in a circle. To heat 12 rolls, microwave on 70% power 1–1½ minutes.

Shrimp Mould
A tasty appetizer that is very attractive on a buffet table

425g (1lb) small shrimps
225g (8oz) cream cheese
1 can (10.4oz) shrimp soup or crab bisque
2 × 15ml tbsp (2tbsp) tomato ketchup
150ml (6fl oz) mayonnaise
4 × 15ml tbsp (4tbsp) green

pepper, diced
4 × 15ml tbsp (4tbsp) celery, diced
3 × 15ml tbsp (3tbsp) onion, grated
1 sachet gelatine (use 1½ sachets gelatine if mould won't be eaten quickly)

Cover and cook shrimps for 3–4½ minutes until they turn pink and opaque, and set aside. Microwave soup for 1–2 minutes on HIGH. Soften cream cheese on 70% power 45 seconds. Soften gelatine in 2 × 15ml tbsp (2tbsp) of cold water and add cream cheese and soup. Stir well, adding remaining ingredients. Pour in fish mould and chill until serving time.

Decorations for making Fish Mould:
It is necessary to make a clear gelatine glaze first to pour in fish mould so raw vegetables will stay in place.

1 Garnish inside of mould by using radish slices for fish scales, olive slices for eyes, strips of carrots, green pepper or thinly sliced celery for fins.
2 Soften 1 sachet gelatine in 50ml (2fl oz) water. Add 225ml (8fl oz) water and microwave on HIGH 1–2 minutes to dissolve gelatine. Gently spoon a little gelatine mixute into mould. Refrigerate to set. Slowly build up gelatine in mould until all is used. Then pour shrimp mixture over glaze and refrigerate until set.

Sugared Pecans or Walnuts

225g (8oz) pecan or walnut halves	50g (2oz) sugar
15g (½oz) butter	1 × 2.5ml tsp (½tsp) cinnamon

Melt butter in a 22.5cm (9in) pie plate. Sir in pecan or walnut halves, sugar and cinnamon and cook for 2 minutes on HIGH. Stir and cook for 2 more minutes. Reduce power to 70% and microwave 1–1½ additional minutes.

Herbed Cream Cheese Mould
Prepare a week before the party to blend flavours.
Refrigerate

225g (8oz) cream cheese	1 × 5ml tsp (1tsp) garlic salt
65ml (2½fl oz) sour cream	Freshly ground pepper
3 × 15ml tbsp (3tbsp) spring onion, chopped	1 × 5ml tsp (1tsp) dried tarragon
4 × 15ml tbsp (4tbsp) parsley	1 × 5ml tsp (1tsp) chives

Soften cheese for 1½–2 minutes at 50% power. Add remaining ingredients and mix well. Pour into mould and chill. Serve with biscuits or Melba toast.
    Garnish as desired.

Low-calorie Stuffed Mushrooms

225g (8oz) large mushrooms
3 medium spring onions
2 × 5ml tsp (2tsp) sour cream
1 × 5ml tsp (1tsp) lemon juice
1 × 2.5ml tsp (½tsp) seasoned
garlic salt

Remove stems from mushrooms and chop finely. Thinly slice spring onions including tops. Mix with mushroom stems. Microwave on HIGH for 2–3 minutes. Add sour cream, lemon juice and garlic salt. Fill mushroom caps and place 10–12 filled caps in pie dish. Microwave for 2–3 minutes on 80% power.

Artichoke Dip
So easy to prepare and so delicious

1 × 400g (14oz) can artichoke
  hearts
225ml (8fl oz) mayonnaise
100g (4oz) grated Parmesan cheese
1 × 15ml tbsp (1tbsp) lemon juice,
optional
2 garlic cloves, crushed
1 × 2.5ml tsp (½tsp) pepper,
  white preferred
Salt

Drain artichokes well, squeezing out all juice. Chop into small pieces. Add remaining ingredients and place in 20cm (8in) square casserole. Cook on HIGH 2 minutes. Stir and cook 5–7 minutes at 50% power. Allow to stand 5 minutes before serving. Then serve hot with Melba toast rounds or other biscuits.

Crab Stuffed Mushrooms

450g (1lb) large mushrooms
40g (1oz) butter
1 × 15ml tbsp (1tbsp) flour
100ml (4fl oz) milk
Salt and white pepper to taste
4 spring onions, finely chopped
150g (6oz) frozen crabmeat,
  thawed
1 × 15ml tbsp (1tbsp) dry sherry
  or dry white wine
1 egg yolk
40g (1½oz) Parmesan cheese

Remove mushroom stems and set aside. Microwave mushroom caps, hollow side down in baking dish for 3–5 minutes on HIGH. Drain, add 15g (½oz) butter and toss.

Make white sauce. Melt 15g (½oz) butter, add 1 × 15ml tbsp (1tbsp) flour and stir to blend. Add milk and cook on 70% power for 1 minute, stirring once. Add salt, pepper, egg yolk, sherry or wine and Parmesan cheese. Stir and add crabmeat. Set aside.

Microwave spring onions for 1 minute on HIGH. Add to crabmeat mixture. Stuff mushroom caps and sprinkle with additional Parmesan cheese if desired. Microwave 8–10 minutes on 70% power, or until hot. Serve at once.

Pecan or Walnut Worcestershire
Delicious with a Bloody Mary!

15g (½oz) butter
2 × 15ml tbsp (2tbsp) Worcestershire sauce

1 dash Tabasco
Salt and pepper to taste
225g (8oz) pecan or walnut halves

Melt butter in a 22.5cm (9in) pie plate. Add Worcestershire sauce, Tabasco and pecan or walnut halves, stirring to coat nuts. Cook for 5–6 minutes on HIGH, stirring every two minutes, making sure nuts from outside are moved to the centre. Salt and pepper to taste and allow to stand 5–10 minutes before serving.

Cheese and Sour Cream Fondue

6 slices bacon
3 × 15ml tbsp (3tbsp) finely chopped onion
2 × 5ml tsp (2tsp) flour

1 × 5ml tsp (1tsp) Worcestershire sauce
450g (1lb) mature Cheddar cheese, grated
400ml (16fl oz) sour cream

Microwave bacon 6–8 minutes at 100% power. Reserve 1 × 15ml tbsp (1tbsp) of bacon fat and sauté onions 45 seconds on HIGH. Stir in flour and add remaining ingredients. Microwave on 50% power for 9–12 minutes until cheese melts. Pour into fondue pot. Top with bacon and place over fondue burner.

'Do Your Own Thing Dip'
Use fresh vegetables as dippers for this tasty appetizer

225g (8oz) cream cheese
1 × 100ml (4fl oz) sour cream or
salad dressing

2–3 chopped spring onions
1 × 2.5ml tsp (½tsp) white pepper

Microwave cream cheese in glass mixing bowl about 2 minutes on
70% power. Add sour cream or salad dressing along with spring
onions and white pepper.

Variation:
Hot Vegetable Dip: Add 100g (4oz) chopped fresh broccoli or
spinach, 100g (4oz) finely chopped fresh mushrooms, 5 slices
crumbled bacon, 50g (2oz) finely grated Parmesan cheese and
1 × 15ml tbsp (1tbsp) fresh lemon juice. Mix well with above
cream cheese mixture. Microwave for 2–3 minutes on 70% power
until warm, allowing flavours to blend.

Devilled Mushrooms

12 appetizers
12 medium mushrooms (3.75cm
  (1½in))
100g (4oz) minced ham
2 ×15ml tbsp (2tbsp) chopped
  shallots
2 × 15ml tbsp (2tbsp) green
  pepper
1 × 15ml tbsp (1tbsp) prepared
  mustard
2 × 5ml tsp (2tsp) mayonnaise

25g (1oz) butter
Dash of pepper
Green olives, sliced, for garnish

Remove mushroom stems (not needed here, so save for use later)
and place mushroom caps in a 22.5cm (9in) glass dish. Cover and
microwave 1–2 minutes on HIGH. Drain. Sprinkle with salt and
add ham, shallots, green pepper, mustard, mayonnaise, butter and
pepper. Mix and spoon into mushroom caps topping with green
olive slices. Cook on HIGH for 2½–3 minutes. Let stand 2 or 3
minutes. Place on platter, garnish and serve immediately.

Wrapped Chicken Livers

20 appetizers

100ml (4fl oz) medium-dry sherry
1 × 5ml tsp (1tsp) dry mustard
Dash of hot pepper sauce

1 × 2.5ml tsp (½tsp) salt
10 chicken livers (325g (¾lb))
10 slices bacon, cut in half

Cut livers in half and marinate in a mixture of sherry, mustard, hot pepper sauce and salt. Cover with clingfilm and let set for several hours in the refrigerator. Stir several times. Cook bacon for 3–4 minutes on HIGH. Drain liver and wrap bacon around each piece, securing with wooden cocktail sticks. Arrange 10 appetizers around edge of plate and cook on HIGH for 3–4 minutes. Repeat process with remaining appetizers.

Cheese Stuffed Mushrooms

450g (1lb) small fresh mushrooms
225g (½lb) cheese, grated
50g (2oz) breadcrumbs
15g (½oz) butter

1 × 5ml tsp (1tsp) dried parsley
White wine
White pepper

Remove mushroom stems and cut into small pieces. Sauté in 15g (½oz) butter. Add dried parsley. Cook on HIGH for 2 minutes. Mix in cheese, breadcrumbs and pepper. Add about 1 × 15ml tbsp (1tbsp) wine to moisten. Stuff mushroom caps and place in circular position to cook. If preparing all mushrooms at one time, cook on HIGH for 8–10 minutes or until hot and cheese melts.

Cheese Bites
A quick appetizer for unexpected guests

Serves 8

6–8 muffins
100g (4oz) chopped black olives
100g (4oz) mature Cheddar cheese
  grated

4 × 15ml tbsp (4tbsp) grated
  onion
1 × 2.5ml tsp (½tsp) curry powder
Salt

Top muffins with well mixed cheese mixture. Place muffins on a paper-towel-lined container. Microwave for 3–4 minutes on 80% power until bubbly. Cut into quarters and serve.

Spicy Meat Balls

3 dozen appetizers

450g (1lb) lean minced beef
1 medium sized onion, finely
  chopped
2 × 15ml tbsp (2tbsp) green
  pepper, finely chopped

1 egg, beaten
2 × 15ml tbsp (2tbsp) milk
50g (2oz) breadcrumbs
1 × 5ml tsp (1tsp) garlic salt
1 × 2.5ml tsp (½tsp) black pepper

Sauce:

325ml (12fl oz) tomato purée
50g (2oz) dark brown sugar
1 × 15ml tbsp (1tbsp) mustard

2 × 15ml tbsp (2tbsp) vinegar
1 × 15ml tbsp (1tbsp)
  Worcestershire sauce

In a large bowl combine beef, onion, green pepper, egg, milk, breadcrumbs, garlic salt and pepper. Toss lightly until mixed. Form into about 3 dozen meat balls. Place in a baking dish in a single layer. Microwave uncovered on 70% power for 3–5 minutes. Stir to rearrange bringing the meatballs on the outside to the centre. Cook on 70% power 2-3 additional minutes until just done. (Some meat balls may still be pink but will finish cooking upon standing.) Drain and cover with foil.

While meat stands combine the sauce ingredients. Microwave sauce for 3–4 minutes on HIGH power. Add sauce to meatballs and cook on 70% power 3–5 minutes stirring once.

Swiss Cheese Fondue
A fun dish to serve for a crowd

450g (1lb) cheese, grated
400ml (16fl oz) dry white wine
Dash of nutmeg
2 × 15ml tbsp (2tbsp) cornflour

3 × 15ml tbsp (3tbsp) Kirsh or
  4 × 15ml tbsp (4tbsp) cognac
2 garlic cloves
1 × 2.5ml tsp (½tsp) salt and
  paprika

Rub cooking utensil with crushed garlic. Pour in wine and microwave at HIGH power for 3–4 minutes, or just before boiling. Add cheese by the handful, stirring to mix well. Microwave on 70% power for 3–6 minutes until cheese melts. Dissolve cornflour in Kirsch or cognac and add to fondue. Mix in nutmeg, salt and paprika. Serve with French bread.

Apple Cheese Ball
A very tasty change

325g (12oz) cream cheese
1 apple, unpeeled
4 spring onions, finely sliced
1 × 2.5ml tsp (½tsp) salt
White pepper
2 × 15ml tbsp (2tbsp) apple juice

75g–100g (3–4oz) grated Cheddar
  cheese
75g (3oz) chopped walnuts
3 × 15ml tbsp (3tbsp) fresh
  parsley, finely chopped

Microwave cream cheese in glass mixing bowl for 1½–2 minutes on 70% power until softened. Core apple and chop into small pieces. Add chopped apple, onion, salt, pepper and apple juice to cream cheese. Microwave for 2–4 minutes on 50% power to blend flavours. Add Cheddar cheese and chill for easier shaping. Form into ball and roll in chopped parsley and nuts.

Mystery Cheese Ball

325g (12oz) cream cheese
225g (8oz) extra strong cheese
100g (¼lb) blue cheese
50g (2oz) chopped parsley
150g (6oz) chopped pecans or
  walnuts

1 garlic clove, crushed
3 × 15ml tbsp (3tbsp)
  Worcestershire sauce
Pinch of Cayenne

Microwave cream cheese for 2 minutes on 50% power to soften slightly. Add half the parsley and half the nuts, along with remaining ingredients. Form into ball, and then roll the ball in the remaining nuts and parsley.

Toast bread for hot sandwiches conventionally because bread will have more body and won't get soggy during heating.

When cooking popcorn in the microwave do so only in popcorn popper designed for the microwave. (Otherwise there is danger of fire.)

21

Spiced Tea

Serves 10

6 whole cloves	1 stick cinnamon
850ml (1½pt) water	3 × 5ml tsp (3tsp) tea, heaped
250ml (½pt) orange juice	225ml (8fl oz) pineapple juice
3 × 15ml tbsp (3tbsp) lemon juice	125g (5oz) sugar

Place cinnamon and cloves in 500ml (¾pt) water and microwave on HIGH 5 minutes. Simmer at 50% power 5 additional minutes. Strain. Make tea in other two cups of water by heating until water boils. Let steep 5 minutes before straining. Add remaining ingredients and heat on HIGH for 14–16 minutes.

Cranberry Punch

Serves 15

1 litre (1¾pt) cranberry juice	65g (2½oz) brown sugar
1 litre (1¾pt) unsweetened pine-apple juice	1 × 5ml tsp (1tsp) whole allspice
	2 cinnamon sticks
500ml (¾pt) water	1 lemon, quartered

Tie spices in cheese cloth (or strain later) and place all ingredients in microwave-proof dish. Microwave on HIGH 24 minutes and 50% power 10 additional minutes.

Hot Cocoa

Serves 5 to 6

850ml (1½pt) milk
250ml (½pt) boiling water
4 × 15ml tbsp (4tbsp) cocoa
100g (4oz) sugar
a few drops vanilla essence

Combine cocoa and sugar in 2 litre (3½pt) glass measure or simmering pot. Add water and mix to blend. Microwave on HIGH for 3 to 4 minutes. Stir occasionally until syrup boils.

Add milk and cook on HIGH until mixture is hot but not boiling. Stir in vanilla and beat with wire whisk. Serve at once.

Hot Scotch
Kids love it!

1 mug of milk

1–2 × 15ml tbsp (1–2 tbsp) butterscotch, broken into small pieces

Heat a mug of milk 1–1½ minutes on HIGH. Add butterscotch and stir. Garnish with a marshmallow and enjoy it!

Hot Tomato Bouillon
Great on a cold day

14 small cups
1 15oz can tomato soup
1 15oz can beef broth
1 397g (13½oz) can tomato juice
1 169g (6oz) can V8 juice
1 × 5ml tsp (1tsp) seasoned salt

Pinch of thyme
1 × 2.5ml tsp (½tsp) creamed horseradish
1 × 15ml tbsp (1tbsp) Worcestershire sauce

Place all ingredients into large simmering pot and heat to blend flavours. Serve hot.

Café Brulot

Serves 8 to 10
1 × 10cm (4in) cinnamon stick
12 whole cloves
Peel of 1 orange cut in 1 spiral piece
Peel of 1 lemon cut in 1 spiral piece

6 × 5ml tsp (6tsp) sugar
150ml (6oz) brandy
50ml (2oz) Triple Sec or Cointreau
1 litre (1¾pt) strong black coffee

In large container add cinnamon, cloves, orange and lemon peel, sugar and Triple Sec. Heat to simmer and carry to table. Add brandy; set aflame and stir until sugar is dissolved. Gradually add hot black coffee and continue mixing until flame flickers. Serve hot in small cups.

Add marshmallows to cocoa during the last 15 seconds of heating. Children enjoy watching this process.

Bloody Mary

2 litres (3½pt) tomato juice
Juice of 4 lemons
Tabasco sauce to taste
5 × 15ml tbsp (5tbsp)
   Worcestershire sauce

2 beef stock cubes
4 × 5ml tsp (4tsp) seasoned salt
850ml (1½pt) Vodka
   (optional)

Heat crumbled stock cubes in 500ml (¾pt) of tomato juice until dissolved for 4 to 5 minutes. Mix with remaining ingredients. Good with or without vodka.

Christmas Wassail

Serves 20
225g (8oz) sugar
1 lemon sliced thinly
450ml (16fl oz) orange juice
100ml (4fl oz) lemon juice

4 sticks cinnamon
450ml (16fl oz) pineapple juice
1.5 litre (2½pt) red wine
225ml (8fl oz) dry sherry

Microwave sugar, cinnamon sticks and lemon slices in ½ cup water for 1 minute on HIGH and 4–5 minutes at 50% power. Strain and add to remaining ingredients.

   Store until guests arrive and heat in cup as needed, garnishing with lemon or orange slices. Microwave 1 cup on HIGH 1½–2 minutes.

🦃 To make the best lemonade, prepare syrup the day before serving. In a 1 litre (1¾pt) container dissolve 325g (12oz) sugar and 1 × 15ml tbsp (1tbsp) finely grated lemon peel with 325ml (12fl oz) water in the microwave for 3–4 minutes on HIGH power. Add 325ml (12fl oz) lemon juice and refrigerate until serving time. To make lemonade, mix 50ml (2fl oz) syrup with 300ml (6fl oz) cold water (or soda water). Makes 16 servings.

🦃 When stirring instant cocoa, tea, or coffee into water boiled in the microwave, put a small amount of mix in first and stir, thus preventing foaming over the top of the cup.

Mulled Cider

Serves 10
1 litre (1¾pt) brewed tea
1 litre (1¾pt) dry cider
100g (4oz) brown sugar
1 cinnamon stick
1 × 5ml tsp (1tsp) whole allspice
1 × 5ml tsp (1tsp) whole cloves

Microwave sugar and half the cider about 5 minutes on HIGH to dissolve sugar. Add remaining ingredients. Microwave on HIGH 16 to 18 minutes. Strain spices. Pour into cider bowl and garnish with baked apples.

Cut skin from 4 apples in flower design and microwave on HIGH 4 to 6 minutes. Stud apples with cloves and float apples in mulled cider bowl.

Hot Buttered Rum
A great warmer-upper for a cold day

150ml (6fl oz) apple juice per mug   1 × 5ml tsp (1tsp) butter
1 tot dark rum   Dash of cinnamon per mug

Place apple juice in mug and heat to boiling. Add rum, butter and cinnamon. Garnish with thinly sliced lemon and cinnamon stick.

🐾 Save left-over coffee and microwave cup by cup as needed. There will be no bitter after-taste.

Simply Scrumptious
Soups, Salads, and Sandwiches

Soups – General Guidelines

Conventional soups must be cooked over low heat and stirred often to prevent sticking, but most can be microwaved on HIGH to the boiling point or serving temperature 70°C (160°F.) The temperature probe is helpful to prevent over-heating, especially with cream soups. Another big plus is that it is easy to clean!

Mushrooms, clams, or other sensitive ingredients may need to cook at 70% power, or lower, to prevent popping.

Generally you should: cook soups covered, sauté vegetables to tenderise before adding to soup, and trim fat from meat so that the soup is not too greasy.

Microwave soups in a container with twice the volume of the ingredients so the mixture does not boil over. Milk 'boils higher' in the microwave than boiled conventionally.

Cream soups sometimes need more thickening than the conventional recipe because there is less moisture evaporation during cooking.

Soup mix containing dehydrated rice or noodles needs to be cooked on a lower setting of 50% to allow the starch to rehydrate and soften.

Stock recipes and soups that require long, slow cooking to blend flavours or tenderise meat are offered in the Clay Pot Cookery chapter.

Home-made Vegetable Soup

100g (4oz) sweetcorn
100g (4oz) sliced green beans
225g (8oz) cabbage, thinly sliced
100g (4oz) carrots, thinly slices
900g (32oz) can tomato juice, or plain tomatoes
50g (2oz) bacon fat

500ml (1pt) chicken stock (preferably home-made)
1 × 15ml tbsp (1tbsp) sugar
1 × 5ml tsp (1tsp) pepper
1 × 5ml tsp (1tsp) basil
2 × 5ml tsp (2tsp) salt

Place all fresh vegetables in large container and cover tightly (clingfilm may be used). Microwave 8–12 minutes on HIGH until done. Stir once or twice. Add remaining ingredients and cook on HIGH 15 minutes. Stir and cook covered 25–30 minutes on 50% POWER. Taste and adjust seasonings.

Crab Soup

1 medium onion, chopped
450g (1lb) white crabmeat
2.5 litres (4½pt) milk
100g (4oz) butter

Salt, pepper and Worcestershire sauce to taste
1 × 5ml tsp (1tsp) cornflour
100g (¼lb) crab roe, chopped
100ml (4fl oz) dry sherry

Sauté onion and butter on HIGH 1–3 minutes. Add crabmeat, milk with cornflour dissolved in it and seasonings. Cook on HIGH just to boiling. Add crab roe and sherry. Stir together well. Sprinkle a little paprika on each serving and serve piping hot.

 For added interest, cut croûtons in shapes.

Salmon Chowder

1 large can salmon (bone and skin removed)
1 large baking potato
1 large onion, thinly sliced
50g (2oz) butter
1 litre (1¾pt) milk (or single cream)
Salt and pepper to taste

Microwave potato 4–6 minutes on HIGH. Sauté onion in butter 1–2 minutes on HIGH. Peel and dice potatoes. Add all ingredients to onion and heat on HIGH to serving temperature.

Oyster Stew: Substitute one 280g (10oz) can oysters (undrained) for salmon and add a dash of celery salt.

Tomato Bisque

Serves 4 to 6
1 large can tomatoes (use fresh ones when in season)
400ml (16fl oz) single cream
1 × 5ml tsp (1tsp) chicken stock granules
1 × 2.5ml tsp (½tsp) basil*
Pinch of onion powder
Pinch of bicarbonate of soda

Put tomatoes, including liquid, in blender and blend a few seconds to chop desired amount. Add all ingredients and microwave on HIGH to serving temperature, about 5 minutes.

*You may substitute sage for basil, if you prefer.

French Onion Soup

Serves 4
4 large onions, thinly sliced
50g (2oz) butter
250ml (½pt) beef stock
750ml (1¼pt) home-made chicken stock, if possible (it is well worth the time and effort. See page 113 for recipe)
50ml (2fl oz) sherry or white wine
1 × 2.5ml tsp (½tsp) white or black pepper (white preferred)

2 slices boiled ham, sliced in thin strips (optional)
325g (12oz) cheese, grated
50g (2oz) Parmesan cheese

28

Combine onion and butter in large casserole. Cover with clingfilm and microwave on HIGH for 6–10 minutes, until onions are semi-soft and translucent. Pour beef and chicken stock over onions. Add ham and microwave 5–7 minutes until heated. Add sherry or wine. Ladle into 4 individual casseroles. Sprinkle with cheeses and microwave 6–8 minutes on HIGH. Serve with toasted French bread.

Chicken and Artichoke Soup
Good appetizer soup

Serves 6

3 shallots
2 cloves garlic
50g (2oz) butter
4 × 15ml tbsp (4tbsp) flour
400ml (16fl oz) chicken stock
1 can artichoke hearts with liquid

2 × 5ml tsp (2tsp) dried parsley
1 bay leaf
Pinch of thyme
225ml (8fl oz) single cream
100g–150g (4–6oz) chicken, cooked and finely chopped

Sauté shallots, garlic and butter on HIGH 2 minutes. Add flour to make a roux. Add stock and cream. Cook on HIGH about 1½ minutes, until thickened. Stir and continue cooking on HIGH 2–4 minutes, just to boiling. Add spices, artichoke hearts and chicken. Heat to serving temperature.

Quick Potato Soup

225g (8oz) sliced, peeled potatoes (raw)
50g (2oz) finely chopped leeks or onions
225ml (8fl oz) water
325ml (12fl oz) single cream

15g (½oz) butter
1 × 2.5ml tsp (½tsp) salt
Pepper
4 thin slices cheese (optional)
Bacon or chives for garnish

Microwave potatoes, onion and water on HIGH 8–10 minutes until potatoes are tender. Cover and let rest 5 minutes. Mash potatoes with a fork. Add remaining ingredients except cheese and cook on HIGH 5–8 minutes to serving temperature. Garnish with cheese and bacon, or chives.

Vichyssoise: Blend Quick Potato Soup in blender till smooth and chill. Serve garnished generously with chives.

Chowder: A variety of delicious chowders may be made by adding 100g (4oz) of chicken or the vegetable of your choice to Quick Potato Soup.

Soup Supreme
Has a delicious flavour

50g (2oz) butter
1 small carrot, peeled and finely
  chopped
1 small stalk celery, finely chopped
½ onion, sliced in thin rings
50g (2oz) finely grated Cheddar
  cheese (medium or mature)

50g (2oz) flour
400ml (16fl oz) chicken stock
400ml (16fl oz) milk
50g (2oz) finely chopped ham
  (optional)
Salt and white pepper

Cook butter, carrot, celery and onion covered on HIGH about 1½–2½ minutes, until vegetables are tender. Stir in flour; add milk and stock. Cook on HIGH 5–8 minutes until soup just starts to boil. Season to taste and add cheese and ham. Stir until cheese melts. Return to microwave and cook on HIGH about 1 minute or to serving temperature. Garnish with chives.

Cream Soup Variations

The best cream soups you've ever tasted may be made by using Soup Supreme as a base and adding the desired vegetable. We prefer to have pieces of vegetables in the soup for texture and interest, but, if you prefer, purée the soup in the blender till it is the texture you like. Soup Supreme or cream soups make a tasty sauce or gravy over vegetables, meat, poultry, rice or pasta, too.

Cream of Cauliflower Soup. Add 1 small head cauliflower cut in small florets. Place in a covered dish with 50ml (2fl oz) water and microwave on HIGH 5–10 minutes. Drain well and add to Soup Supreme.

Cream of Broccoli Soup: Microwave 450g (1lb) frozen broccoli on HIGH 8–10 minutes. Drain well and stir into Soup Supreme. Garnish with croûtons.

Cream of Spinach Soup: Add 450g (1lb) frozen, chopped spinach. Microwave frozen spinach on HIGH 8–10 minutes. Drain well and stir into Soup Supreme. Add a dash of tarragon or nutmeg, if desired. Garnish with fried bacon curls, chopped egg, or croutons.

Cream of Carrot Soup: Add 100g (4oz) sliced carrots (make a few carrot curls for garnish), 100g (4oz) cooked rice, 1 × 5ml tsp (1tsp) dried parsley, dash of celery salt and cayenne. Place carrots in covered dish with 2 × 15ml tbsp (2tbsp) water and microwave on HIGH 2–5 minutes. Drain and add with all other ingredients to Soup Supreme.

Cream of Asparagus Soup: Microwave 225g (8oz) frozen asparagus pieces on HIGH 3–5 minutes and add to Soup Supreme.

Cream of Artichoke Soup: Add 1 can drained chopped artichoke hearts to Soup Supreme.

Potato Sausage Soup
A quick hearty supper soup

225g (½lb) sausage
1 chopped onion
50g (2oz) chopped celery
225ml (8fl oz) hot water
1 × 2.5ml tsp (½tsp) rosemary, crushed
Pinch garlic powder

1 × 5ml tsp (1tsp) salt
Pepper
325g (¾lb) straight cut chips (or make your own from fresh potatoes)
325ml (12fl oz) milk
Parsley

Cook sausage, onion and celery on HIGH 4–6 minutes. Drain fat and add water, seasonings and potatoes. Cover and cook on HIGH 10 minutes, until potatoes are tender. Stir in milk and heat to serving temperature. Garnish with parsley.

When converting a conventional soup recipe to microwave, reduce the amount of liquid, unless cooking dried beans or peas. Also reduce the salt and other seasonings.

Cutting meats and vegetables in small pieces of uniform size will help the soup cook more evenly.

Egg Flower Soup

Serves 4 to 6

225g (½lb) lean pork, cut in fine strips
½ onion, chopped
2 eggs, beaten
1.5 litre (2½pt) chicken stock

1 × 15ml tbsp (1tbsp) cornflour and 50ml (2fl oz) water
2 × 15ml tbsp (2tbsp) soy sauce
1 × 5ml tsp (1tsp) sherry
Dash pepper

Sauté onion and pork covered on HIGH 3–5 minutes. Add stock, soy sauce, sherry and pepper. Heat to boiling by cooking on HIGH 6–8 minutes. Slowly dribble beaten egg into boiling soup to form 'flowers'. Add cornflour and water mixture and stir to thicken. Microwave a few minutes longer if needed.

🐦 Frozen bread can be quickly defrosted in the microwave. Approximately 1 minute on 80% power is sufficient for 2 slices of bread. Bread should be wrapped in paper towels or a cloth towel to absorb moisture.

🐦 Microwave soups usually need a little more thickening than conventional recipes.

🐦 Heat single servings of your favourite canned or dried soups in minutes. Microwave on HIGH about 2 minutes per cup. Covering is not necessary but speeds heating time a little.

🐦 Dense purées, cream soups and soups containing less tender cuts of meat should be cooked on a reduced power level.

Salads – General Guidelines

The microwave oven makes salads even better than before. Cooked vegetables will have a prettier colour than ever. Gelatine salads will be smoother. The flavour of meat salads will be better. Salad dressings are quick and easy.

The time factor in making salads is one big advantage. Water can be boiled quickly and cream cheese softened in a wink. Meats can be cooked in a jiffy, and vegetables steamed in a hurry.

Apricot Salad
Good with anything and any time!

1 × 480g (17oz) can apricots,
  drained and quartered (reserve
  juice)
1 × 100g (4oz) bottle maraschino
  cherries, halved (reserve juice)
50ml (2fl oz) cider vinegar

3 sticks cinnamon
1 × 15ml tbsp (1tbsp) whole
  cloves
75g (3oz) gelatine
100g (4oz) nuts, chopped

In a measuring jug add enough water with apricot and cherry juice and vinegar to make 400ml (16fl oz). Add spices. Microwave on HIGH 3 minutes and then turn to 50% power for 7 minutes. Cover and let sit several minutes. Strain liquid. Add gelatine and stir until dissolved. Add fruit and nuts. Pour into mould. Chill.

Ginger Ale Moulded Salad
Especially good with roast pork and ham

2 × 15ml tbsp (2tbsp) gelatine
50ml (2fl oz) water
100ml (4fl oz) orange juice
100g (4oz) sugar
Salt
400ml (16fl oz) ginger-ale
2 × 5ml tsp (2tsp) lemon juice
225g (½lb) grapes, seeded
1 orange, peeled and sliced
1 grapefruit, sectioned
6 slices unsweetened pineapple

3 × 5ml tsp (3tsp) preserved
  ginger, chopped
225g (8fl oz) mayonnaise

Soak gelatine in water. Place orange juice in a large measuring jug. Microwave juice on HIGH for 1–1½ minutes or until orange juice boils. Dissolve gelatine in boiled orange juice. Add sugar, salt, ginger ale and lemon juice. Chill until nearly set. Fold in fruits and ginger. Pour into an oiled 1.5 litre (2½pt) mould. Chill until set. Serve with mayonnaise.

🐄 Allow at least 4 to 6 hours for a mould to set. Overnight setting is best if time is available.

Lettuce and Bacon Salad
Great with fresh lettuce from the garden

Serves 6 to 8

5 slices bacon
3 × 15ml tbsp (3tbsp) bacon fat
50ml (2fl oz) cider vinegar
2 × 15ml tbsp (2tbsp) water
1 × 15ml tbsp (1tbsp) sugar

Pepper
1 × 2.5ml tsp (½tsp) salt
Pinch of dry mustard
1 head lettuce, torn apart
4 spring onions, thinly sliced

Cook bacon in a glass baking dish 4 to 5 minutes on HIGH, or until bacon is crisp. Drain bacon, crumble, and set aside. Combine remaining ingredients, except lettuce and onions, and mix well. Cook 2 to 3 minutes on HIGH or until hot. Pour hot dressings over lettuce and onions in salad bowl. Toss lightly and garnish with crumbled bacon. Serve immediately.

Two chopped hard-boiled eggs are an extra touch.

Mexican Salad

Serves 12

1–4 × 5ml tsp (1–4tsp) chilli
    powder – or to taste
2.5ml tsp (½tsp) garlic salt
450g (1lb) minced chuck steak
1 large head Iceberg lettuce
1 × 395g (15oz) can kidney beans
1 stick celery, chopped
2 tomatoes, diced

10 olives, sliced in rings
½ onion, finely chopped
75g (3oz) strong cheese, coarsely
    grated
1 × 225g (8oz) bottle salad
    dressing
1 small packet potato sticks or
    crisps, crushed

Cook meat, chilli powder and garlic salt on HIGH for 5 to 6 minutes. Drain and rinse kidney beans. Add beans, celery, tomatoes, olives, onion, cheese and dressing to lettuce. Add drained meat. Chill for at least 1 hour. Before serving, add potato sticks or crisps and toss.

🍲 450g (1lb) fresh spinach is a delicious substitute for the lettuce.

🍲 If tossed salads are made in advance, break the lettuce rather than cut the lettuce to prevent browning.

Fresh Cranberry Salad
A great dish with turkey

Serves 8 to 10

450g (1lb) cranberries, ground or minced
1 whole orange, ground or minced
225g (8oz) sugar
2 × 15ml tbsp (2tbsp) gelatine
325ml (12fl oz) hot water

100g (4oz) chopped pecans or walnuts
2 sticks chopped celery
1 × 225g (8oz) can crushed pineapple

Combine ground cranberries, orange and sugar. Let mixture sit overnight. Microwave water 2 minutes on HIGH and add gelatine stirring to dissolve. When mixture starts to set, add remaining ingredients and mix thoroughly. Pour into oiled salad mould. Refrigerate until set. Serve on lettuce leaves with mayonnaise.

Fresh Spinach Salad

6 slices bacon
225g (½lb) mushrooms, thinly sliced
450g (1lb) spinach, washed
3 spring onions, sliced

2 × 15ml tbsp (2tbsp) oil
4 × 15ml tbsp (4tbsp) lemon juice
2 × 15ml tbsp (2tbsp) vinegar
Salad tomatoes
Salt and pepper

Microwave bacon 6 to 8 minute on HIGH. Remove bacon. Add onions to bacon fat. Microwave 1 to 2 minutes on HIGH or until onions are soft. Add oil, lemon juice and vinegar to onion mixture. Pour over spinach, mushrooms and tomatoes. Toss in crumbled bacon. Add salt and pepper to taste. Serve at once.

Layered Potato Salad
A layered potato salad with mustard sauce

6 medium potatoes, cooked and sliced
2 onions, sliced and divided in rings
3 hard-boiled eggs, chopped
100g (4oz) olives, sliced

Mustard Sauce:
125ml (¼pt) mayonnaise
1–2 × 15ml tbsp (1–2tbsp) made mustard
Vinegar to taste

Microwave 6 potatoes on HIGH 15 to 18 minutes or until slightly firm. Wrap in foil or cover with a bowl 5 to 10 minutes. Cool. Peel and slice. Place a layer of potatoes, onions, eggs and olives in a dish. Dribble mustard sauce over vegetables. Layer and dribble with more sauce. Chill and serve.

Picnic Vegetable Salad

Serves 15 to 18

1 bunch broccoli
225g (8oz) fresh mushrooms
1 head cauliflower

1 × 225ml (8fl oz) bottle Italian
   dressing (see page 38)

Cut broccoli into florets and cook 2–3 minutes on HIGH in a covered casserole dish. Cool. Slice mushrooms, break up cauliflower and put in bowl. Add cooled broccoli. Add bottle of Italian dressing. Toss thoroughly. Cool in refrigerator for several hours.

German Potato Salad
A delicious hot salad

Serves 6 to 8

6 medium potatoes
6 slices bacon, drained
1 medium onion, sliced thinly
2 × 15ml tbsp (2tbsp) flour
3 × 15ml tbsp (3tbsp) sugar

1 × 5ml tsp (1tsp) celery seed
1 × 2.5ml tsp (½tsp) pepper
150ml (6fl oz) water
50ml–75ml (2–3fl oz) vinegar
Salt

Microwave potatoes on HIGH for 15 to 18 minutes and allow to stand wrapped in foil for 10 minutes. Cook bacon on HIGH for 6 to 9 minutes or until crisp. Drain bacon, reserving fat. Place onion slices in dish with fat and cook 2 to 3 minutes. Add flour, sugar, salt, celery seed and pepper, stirring to blend. Add water and vinegar. Cook on HIGH 2 to 3 minutes. Peel and slice potatoes. Add to sauce and cook until hot. Crumble bacon and sprinkle over top. Serve hot.

🐀 When using gelatine, dissolve 1 envelope in 4 × 15ml tbsp (4tbsp) cold water. Let gelatine sit until it gels. After it gels, place it in the microwave on HIGH for 30 to 40 seconds.

Yummy Chicken Salad
A good luncheon salad

Serves 6 to 8

675g (1½lb) cooked chicken, cubed
1 can mandarin oranges, drained
1 stick celery, chopped
25g (1oz) slivered almonds

100g (¼lb) seedless white grapes, halved
65ml (2½fl oz) mayonnaise
65ml (2½fl oz) sour cream
Salt and pepper to taste

Cook chicken in microwave. Combine chicken, celery, oranges, grapes and almonds in mixing bowl. In separate bowl blend mayonnaise and sour cream, add to chicken mixture and stir well to blend all ingredients. Chill well and serve.

Ever-ready Coleslaw
Keeps 2 to 3 weeks in the refrigerator

Serves 8 to 10

150ml (6fl oz) oil
225g (8oz) sugar
225ml (8fl oz) cider vinegar
1 × 5ml tsp (1tsp) celery seeds

1 × 5ml tsp (1tsp) mustard seeds
1 × 2.5ml tsp (½tsp) turmeric
1 × 5ml tsp (1tsp) salt

Place ingredients in container and microwave 3 to 4 minutes on HIGH or until mixture boils. Cool and pour over the following vegetables:

1 medium cabbage, chopped
1 medium green pepper, chopped

1 medium onion, chopped
1 small jar pimento, chopped

Chill and serve.

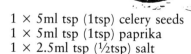

Sweet and Sour Dressing

150g (6oz) sugar
100ml (4fl oz) vinegar
225ml (8fl oz) oil

1 × 5ml tsp (1tsp) celery seeds
1 × 5ml tsp (1tsp) paprika
1 × 2.5ml tsp (½tsp) salt

Combine sugar and vinegar in glass measuring jug. Microwave 2 to 3 minutes on HIGH until mixture begins to boil. Add remaining ingredients and mix well. Chill.

Creamy Bacon Dressing
Tasty on green Salads

4 slices bacon
1 egg, well beaten
100ml (4fl oz) sour cream

100ml (4fl oz) cider vinegar
2 × 15ml tbsp (2tbsp) sugar
3 spring onions, thinly sliced

Cook bacon on HIGH 3 to 5 minutes or until crisp. Drain bacon and crumble. Cool bacon fat. In a small dish, beat the egg and add the sour cream, vinegar, sugar and onion. Stir the mixture into the cool bacon fat. Microwave 3 to 4 minutes on 70% power or until thickened, stirring every minute. Add bacon and serve.

Marinated Asparagus Salad
This is a great Italian dressing, too!

450g (1lb) fresh asparagus
2 onions sliced in rings

225g (½lb) fresh mushrooms,
sliced

Italian Dressing:
65ml (2½fl oz) cider vinegar
1 × 15ml tbsp (1tbsp) sugar
2 × 15ml tbsp (2tbsp) lemon juice
1 × 5ml tsp (1tsp) garlic salt
1 × 2.5ml tsp (½tsp) dry mustard

1 × 2.5ml tsp (½tsp) oregano
Pinch of basil
225ml (8fl oz) vegetable oil
Freshly ground black pepper

Place vinegar in measuring jug and microwave on HIGH for 30 seconds or until vinegar is hot. Add sugar, lemon juice and spices and stir. Add oil and blend well. Cook asparagus in tightly covered dish. Microwave on HIGH 2–3 minutes. Drain and cool. Add onions and mushrooms to asparagus and cover with Italian dressing.

Marinated Fruit Bowl

1 cantaloupe melon, peeled and cut
   in pieces
1 can cherries, drained

150g–225g (6–8oz) blackberries,
   drained and rinsed
3 fresh peaches, peeled

Use any combination of fruits, especially fresh fruit in season.

Marinade:

100g (4oz) sugar
150ml (6fl oz) water
2 × 15ml tbsp (2tbsp) fresh lime
   juice

Sprig of mint
Pinch of aniseed, optional
Pinch of salt

Place marinade ingredients in measuring jug. Microwave on HIGH 3½ minutes. Cover and steep 10 minutes. Cool. Pour over fruit and chill 2 hours or longer.

Sandwiches – General Guidelines

Sandwiches are a very versatile food item. They can go almost anywhere – picnics, snack suppers or a main dish. The microwave can make sandwiches fast, tasty and simple.

Use firm, thick slices of bread for microwave sandwiches.

Toast or day-old bread is a good choice.

Sandwich fillings and spreads should be cooked separately. The bread will become chewy and tough if cooked at the same time as the fillings.

Reheating sandwiches is easy in the microwave. Wrap sandwich in paper towel and reheat.

Reuben

Serves 4

8 slices rye bread, toasted
4 slices cheese
4 slices corned beef

4 × 15ml tbsp (4tbsp) sauerkraut,
   well drained
4 × 15ml tbsp (4tbsp) Thousand
   Island dressing

Arrange 4 slices of bread on a paper towel. Top each slice of bread with a piece of cheese, 1 slice of corned beef, 1 × 15ml tbsp (1tbsp) sauerkraut, and 1 × 15ml tbsp (1tbsp) dressing. Microwave 70% power 5 to 7 minutes, or until cheese starts to melt. Top with remaining slices of bread.

Sloppy Joes
A favourite with teenagers

Serves 8

450g (1lb) minced beef
2 × 15ml tbsp (2tbsp) onion, finely chopped
1 × 15ml tbsp (1tbsp) celery, finely chopped
1 × 15ml tbsp (1tbsp) green pepper, finely chopped

1 × 2.5ml tsp (½tsp) salt
Pepper
1 × 5ml tsp (1tsp) Worcestershire sauce
225ml (8fl oz) barbecue or chilli sauce
8 hamburger buns

Placed minced beef, onion, celery and green pepper in a dish. Microwave on HIGH 7 minutes. Drain off excess liquid. Add spices and sauce. Cook 8–10 minutes covered on 50% power. Spoon over hamburger buns.

Italian Sausage Sandwiches

Serves 6

450g (1lb) Italian sausage, sliced 6mm (¼in) thick*
½ onion, sliced in rings
1 green pepper, cut in strips
2 tomatoes, peeled and sliced

Pinch of salt
Pinch of oregano
50g (2oz) Mozzarella cheese, grated
6 French rolls, toasted and split

Microwave Italian sausage on HIGH for 5–8 minutes. Drain well. Add vegetables and cover. Cook 3 to 4 minutes on HIGH or until tender. Stir in seasonings. Spoon on rolls. Sprinkle with cheese. Microwave on 70% power 2–3 minutes till cheese melts.

*Substitute minced pork or beef and flavour to taste like Italian sausage. To do this sauté 2 × 15ml tbsp (2tbsp) oil and 1 × 15ml tbsp (1tbsp) fennel seed for 1 minute on HIGH. Let mixture set for several minutes. Strain and add oil to meat.

Chicken Divan Sandwiches

Serves 6

3 sandwich rolls, split and toasted
6 slices cheese
325g (¾lb) sliced cooked chicken
1 × 283g (10oz) packet frozen
  broccoli, thawed
150ml (6fl oz) mayonnaise

25g (1oz) grated Parmesan cheese
1 × 5ml tsp (1tsp) dry mustard
2–3 × 15ml tbsp (2–3tbsp) milk
2 × 15ml tbsp (2tbsp) onion,
  chopped

Arrange rolls in a dish. Place on rolls: sliced chicken, cheese and broccoli. In a separate bowl, mix thoroughly mayonnaise, cheese, mustard, and gradually stir in milk. Spoon over sandwiches and sprinkle with onions. Microwave on HIGH 5 to 7 minutes, or until broccoli is tender. Cover with clingfilm when cooking.

Simply Scrumptious
Vegetables and Fruit

General Guidelines

Vegetables and fruits cooked in the microwave are Simply Scrumptious! Rapid cooking in a very small amount of water is the best way to retain nutrients and flavour.

An added bonus is the way that vegetables and fruits cooked in the microwave retain colour, texture and taste. To enjoy vegetables and fruits at their peak of goodness, always begin by selecting ones of good quality.

If vegetables and fruits are washed right before cooking, it is usually not necessary to add additional water.

Cover most vegetables tightly with clingfilm to hold in moisture and speed the cooking process. Carefully uncover when removing to prevent burns.

Arrange whole vegetables such as potatoes and beetroot in a ring in the microwave, allowing space between vegetables if possible.

Small pieces of vegetables cook faster and more evenly than larger ones.

Fresh vegetables will microwave faster because they contain more natural moisture.

The density of vegetables affects cooking time. Vegetables such as asparagus or broccoli should be arranged with the tougher stalks to the outside of the dish.

Always prick the skin of whole vegetables such as potatoes or marrow so steam can escape.

Always allow vegetables to stand covered after removing from the microwave so the centre can finish cooking without over-cooking the outside.

Add salt after cooking, or dissolve salt in water before adding to vegetables. This prevents dry or discoloured spots.

Remember that the starting temperature is important. Therefore vegetables and fruits that are chilled take longer to cook than if at room temperature.

Broccoli Tomato Cups
A pretty dish to serve at a dinner party

Serves 6

1 × 283g (10oz) packet frozen chopped broccoli
6 medium-sized fresh tomatoes
50g (2oz) soft breadcrumbs

1 × 2.5ml tsp (½tsp) salt
Pepper
50g (2oz) Parmesan cheese

Place unwrapped broccoli in a dish and microwave on HIGH 5–7 minutes. Let stand covered for 2–3 minutes and drain well. Cut off the stem end of each tomato and scoop out pulp. Set aside. Combine the drained broccoli, bread crumbs, salt, pepper and half of cheese. Fill tomato cups with mixture. Add as much of the tomato pulp as needed to fill all the tomatoes. Arrange in a circle in a baking dish. Cover and microwave on HIGH 4–6 minutes. Sprinkle cheese over top and allow to stand covered several minutes before serving.

Low-calorie Summer Vegetables
Delicious!

Serves 4 to 6

1 medium onion, sliced thinly
1 green pepper, chopped
1 small aubergine, cubed
3 courgettes, sliced
3 tomatoes, cubed
50ml (2fl oz) cooking oil or bacon
    fat

Salt and pepper to taste
1 × 5ml tsp (1tsp) oregano
50g (2oz) Parmesan cheese (for
    variety substitute mature
    Cheddar)

Place all vegetables except tomatoes in baking dish and sprinkle with oregano. Cover tightly with clingfilm. Microwave on HIGH for 6–8 minutes. Stir and check if vegetables are cooked. Add salt, pepper and tomato wedges, stirring to dissolve salt. Cook 1–2 additional minutes. Remove from oven and add cheese. Cover and allow to stand for 5 minutes until cheese melts.

Asparagus Almondine
A taste treat in springtime

Serves 4 to 6

450g (1lb) fresh asparagus spears,
    trimmed and pared
4 × 15ml tbsp (4tbsp) sliced
    almonds

25g (1oz) butter
1 × 15ml tbsp (1tbsp) water
1 × 2.5ml tsp (½tsp) seasoned salt

Microwave almonds and butter in small bowl or glass cup. Cook uncovered on HIGH 4–6 minutes, stirring several times. Place asparagus in glass baking dish, arranging tips in the centre of dish. Add water and cover with clingfilm. Cook on HIGH until almost tender, about 8 minutes. Drain. Sprinkle with toasted buttered almonds and salt.

    Variation· Follow basic cooking directions above. Melt 50g (2oz) butter and add 2 × 15ml tbsp (2tbsp) fresh lemon juice. Pour over asparagus at end of standing time. Add salt and pepper to taste.

    Follow basic cooking directions above, using 50g (2oz) butter and fresh lemon juice. Pour over asparagus and add roasted cashew nuts.

Broccoli Cauliflower Quickie

Serves 6 to 8

2 × 283g (10oz) packets frozen, chopped broccoli, thawed and drained
1 × 283g (10oz) packet cauliflower, thawed

1 × 283g (10oz) can cream of celery soup
1 × 100g (4oz) can mushrooms
1 × 225g (8oz) jar cheese spread
Fried onion rings

Layer vegetables. Mix soup and Cheese spread and pour over top of vegetables. Cover with clingfilm and microwave for 12–18 minutes on HIGH. Add onion rings and cook 1–2 minutes.

Courgettes with Cranberry

Serves 4

450g (1lb) courgettes
2 × 15ml tbsp (2tbsp) brown sugar

1 × 2.5ml tsp (½tsp) cinnamon
1 × 450g (16oz) jar cranberry sauce

Cut courgettes in half and remove seeds. Place in baking dish and sprinkle with brown sugar and cinnamon. Fill with cranberry sauce and cover tightly with clingfilm. Cook on HIGH for 8–10 minutes, or until they can be pierced with a fork easily.

Variations: Follow preceding recipe, substituting chopped apples for cranberry sauce and add one knob of butter to each courgette half. A dash of lemon juice gives added zest.

Courgettes with Parmesan

Serves 4

2 medium-sized courgettes
50g (2oz) butter
50g (2oz) grated Parmesan cheese

Salt to taste and freshly ground black pepper

Cut courgettes in half lengthwise and remove seeds. Place open side up in a baking dish. Sprinkle with salt and pepper. Add butter and cheese. Cover tightly with clingfilm and microwave for 9–10 minutes on HIGH until they can be easily pierced with a fork after standing 5 minutes.

Cabbage and Noodles Delight

Serves 4 to 6

1 small cabbage, shredded
1 medium onion, thinly sliced
50g (2oz) butter
1–2 × 5ml tsp (1–2tsp) poppy
  seeds

Salt and pepper to taste
225g (8oz) medium-sized egg
  noodles, cooked

Combine all ingredients except egg noodles in a casserole. Cook on HIGH 5–7 minutes, stirring midway through cooking time. Stir in noodles.

Garden Fresh Cabbage
Simple and delicious

1 medium-sized head of cabbage   50g (2oz) bacon fat or butter

Wash and cut cabbage into uniform pieces. Cover tightly with clingfilm and microwave for 8–10 minutes on HIGH. Remove from microwave and add bacon fat, butter and salt and pepper.

Variations: Add onion and thin slices of carrots, placing carrots around the outside edge of dish and cook as directed above.

Low-calorie way: Omit bacon fat or butter. Add lemon juice and pepper.

Courgette Casserole

Serves 6 to 8

450g (1lb) courgettes, sliced
1 medium onion, chopped
1 grated carrot
1 × 295g (10.4oz) can condensed
  cream of chicken soup
2 eggs

75g (3oz) mature Cheddar cheese,
  grated
50g (2oz) butter
Salt
Pepper
Seasoned breadcrumbs

Microwave courgettes, onion and grated carrot on HIGH for 8–10 minutes until tender. Drain and add soup, eggs, Cheddar cheese, butter, salt and pepper. Cover tightly with clingfilm and cook for 6–8 minutes on HIGH. Add crumbs to the top of casserole and cook 1–2 additional minutes, uncovered.

Carrot and Cheese Ring

A pretty dish served at a buffet. Fill the centre with
green peas and onions or carrot curls and parsley

Serves 6 to 8

225g (8oz) finely shredded carrots
1 stick of celery, finely diced
100g (4oz) finely chopped onion
50g (2oz) dry breadcrumbs
75g (3oz) shredded mature
   Cheddar cheese

325ml (12fl oz) thick white sauce
   (see page 61)
Salt
Pepper
4 eggs, well beaten

Combine carrots, celery, onions, breadcrumbs, cheese, white sauce, salt and pepper. Beat eggs and add to carrot mixture. Place 1 × 15ml tbsp (1tbsp) breadcrumbs in bottom of oiled 1.5 litre (2½pt) ring mould. (If mould isn't available use a smaller bowl placed in a larger round casserole dish.) Cook for 12–16 minutes on 70% power. Allow to stand 5–10 minutes before emptying out onto serving dish.

Corn on the Cob

Wrap individual ears of husked corn in clingfilm and place in oven, cooking on HIGH 2–3 minutes per ear. Let stand 5 minutes before serving.

If cooking 4 or more ears, it is more practical to place corn in glass baking dish and cover tightly with clingfilm, cooking 2–3 minutes per ear and rearrange once. Butter and enjoy!

Corn in the husk is a tasty delight also. Remove several outside husks and place corn in microwave, cooking on HIGH 2–3 minutes. Remove, let stand a few minutes and pull husks away from corn. The corn silks will follow easily.

Broccoli Cheese Casserole

Serves 4 to 6

125ml (¼pt) milk
3 eggs
25g (1oz) flour
1 × 5ml tsp (1tsp) salt
Pepper
1 medium onion, thinly sliced

1 × 283g (10oz) packet of
  chopped broccoli, thawed and
  drained
75g (3oz) grated cheese
100g (4oz) cottage cheese
  (optional)

Blend milk, eggs, flour, salt and pepper and set aside. Place alternate layers of broccoli, onions and cheese in casserole. Pour egg mixture over layers. Microwave for 10–15 minutes on 70% power. To promote even cooking after 7 minutes, gently stir the mixture towards the centre.

Sweet-sour Green Beans

Serves 4

4 slices bacon, cut up
1 × 452g (16oz) can French green
  beans
1 medium onion, sliced

50g (2oz) sugar
50ml (2fl oz) vinegar
1 × 2.5ml tsp (½tsp) salt
White pepper

Place bacon and onion in a casserole dish. Cover and microwave on HIGH 4–5 minutes, or until onion is tender and bacon cooked, stirring once. Add sugar, vinegar, pepper and beans. Microwave on HIGH 8–10 minutes, stirring midway through. Salt to taste.

Note: Frozen French beans may be substituted for canned. Simply microwave one 452g (1lb) packet for 6–8 minutes or until hot. Drain and add to sweet-sour mixture.

Sweet-sour Carrots
Hungarian-style

Serves 6

450g (1lb) fresh carrots
50ml (2fl oz) water
1 × 5ml tsp (1tsp) salt
2 × 15ml tbsp (2tbsp) butter

100ml (4fl oz) vinegar
150g (6oz) sugar
1 × 15ml tbsp (1tbsp) chopped
  parsley

Wash and scrape carrots, cutting them into 7.5cm × 1.25cm (3 × ½in) strips. Place carrots and water in dish and microwave on HIGH 8–10 minutes until slightly tender. Let stand several minutes and drain water. Add butter, vinegar and sugar and cook 3–5 minutes on HIGH. Salt to taste. Garnish with fresh parsley.

Spinach-stuffed Onions

Serves 8

4 medium onions
450g (1lb) fresh spinach, stems removed
2 × 15ml tbsp (2tbsp) melted butter
50ml (2fl oz) single cream or evaporated milk
Salt and pepper to taste
50g (2oz) Parmesan cheese

Peel onions and cut in halves horizontally. Microwave 6–8 minutes. Cool slightly, remove centre of onions and dice, leaving shells intact. Wash spinach and microwave 1–2 minutes, using only water that clings to leaves. Drain and chop. (Frozen, drained spinach may also be used.) Mix chopped spinach and diced onions, adding melted butter and cream along with salt and pepper. Fill onion shells with spinach and sprinkle generously with cheese. Microwave at 70% power for 5–8 minutes until heated thoroughly.

Cream-style Corn

4 generous servings for corn lovers!

8–10 ears of tender sweetcorn
75g (3oz) butter or bacon fat
100ml (4fl oz) water
100ml (4fl oz) milk
2 × 15ml tbsp (2tbsp) cornflour
Salt and pepper to taste

Cut corn from the cob halfway through kernels, and then scrape remaining corn from each ear, catching all the corn juice. Add water, along with butter or bacon fat and place mixture in baking dish, covering tightly with clingfilm. Cook at HIGH power 7–9 minutes, stirring once. Add cornflour to milk and blend. Add blended mixture to corn, stirring well. Cook at 70% power for 3–5 minutes, stirring once. Add salt and pepper to taste.

Fresh Broccoli with Cheese Sauce

Serves 4 to 6

675g (1½lb) fresh broccoli spears
25g (1oz) butter
2 × 15ml tbsp (2tbsp) flour
225ml (8fl oz) milk

75g (3oz) mature Cheddar cheese
1 × 2.5ml tsp (½tsp) white pepper
Toasted sesame seeds, optional

Trim 2.5cm (1in) from butt end of spears and peel if broccoli appears tough. Arrange spears with tender heads towards centre of dish and cover tightly with clingfilm. Microwave 8–12 minutes on HIGH until pieces can be pierced with fork. Cover and let stand while cheese sauce is prepared.

Melt butter and add flour, stirring until smooth. Add milk and pepper. Cook on 70% power for 4–5 minutes until thickened. Remove from oven and add grated Cheddar cheese, stirring until melted and smooth. Pour over broccoli and add toasted sesame seeds if available. Garnish with slices of tomato if desired.

Aubergine Parmesan

Serves 6

50g (2oz) chopped onion
2 garlic cloves, crushed
15g (½oz) butter or margarine
1 × 424g (15oz) bottle tomato
  sauce
1 × 15ml tbsp (1tbsp) light brown
  sugar
1 × 5ml tsp (1tsp) dried oregano

1 × 2.5ml tsp (½tsp) dried basil
2 × 15ml tbsp (2tbsp) milk
1 egg, beaten
1 medium aubergine, cut into 2cm
  (¾in) thick slices
75g (3oz) dried breadcrumbs
50g (2oz) Parmesan cheese
75g (3oz) grated Mozzarella cheese

Sauté onion and garlic in butter in a covered casserole on HIGH for 2–3 minutes. Add tomato sauce, sugar, oregano and basil. Re-cover and cook on HIGH 3–4 minutes. Stir and reduce power to 50%. Microwave 5–7 minutes or until flavours are blended. Set sauce aside.

Blend eggs and milk together. Dip aubergine slices in egg mixture and then coat with breadcrumbs. Place in 30cm × 20cm (12 × 8in) dish in a single layer, over-lapping edges when needed. Cover loosely with greaseproof paper.

Microwave on HIGH 10–15 minutes or until aubergine is fork tender, rearranging once after half the cooking time. Sprinkle with three-quarters of the Mozzarella cheese. Spoon sauce over and top with remaining Parmesan and Mozarella cheese. Cook on HIGH 1–2 minutes until cheeses melt.

Onion Casserole
Great with steaks!

Servers 4 to 6

3 large onions	1 × 2.5ml tsp (½tsp) white pepper
75g (3oz) butter	1 × 2.5ml tsp (½tsp) salt
50g (2oz) Parmesan cheese	Crisp cream crackers

Peel and thinly slice onions. Place in baking dish and dot with butter. Cover with clingfilm and microwave 3 minutes on HIGH. Stir to distribute butter and cook 5–7 additional minutes. Remove from oven and stir in cheese, salt and pepper. Cover and let stand 5 minutes while cheese melts. Add cracker crumbs to top.

Marrow Parmesan

Serves 4

450g (1lb) thinly sliced baby marrow	1 × 2.5ml tsp (½tsp) salt
1 medium onion, thinly sliced	Pepper
40g (1½oz) butter	25g (1oz) Parmesan cheese

Place marrow, onions and butter in dish and cover lightly with clingfilm. Cook for 8–10 minutes on HIGH until done. Add salt, pepper, and Parmesan. Allow to stand several minutes, letting cheese melt before serving.

Variation: Add 1–2 × 5ml tsp (1–2tsp) of dried dill weed, 1 × 5ml tsp (1tsp) paprika, and 2 × 15ml tbsp (2tbsp) vinegar upon completion of cooking time.

🍆 Aubergine slices: Cut in 12mm (½in) thick slices crosswise. Spread each side with soft butter. Sprinkle with salt, pepper, grated onion and lemon juice. Cook on HIGH for 30–40 seconds per slice.

Garden Fresh Green Beans
Fresh green beans are a must

Serves 4

225g (½lb) green beans (break in uniform pieces)
1 medium onion, thinly sliced

6–8 medium mushrooms, sliced
25g (1oz) butter
Salt to taste

Combine beans, onion, and mushroom slices. Add butter to the top of beans and cover tightly with clingfilm. Cook for 5 minutes on HIGH stirring after 2 minutes of cooking time. Let stand 5 minutes before serving.

Low-calorie Baby Marrow
Very tasty with roast beef

Serves 2

1 × 450g (1lb) baby marrow

Split in half and remove seed. Place cut side down in baking dish. Pierce outside skin several times with fork. Bake for 8–11 minutes on HIGH. Remove from microwave and add a pat of butter, salt, freshly ground black pepper and a dash of nutmeg.

Courgette and Tomato Layer
Low in calories and fast in speed

Serves 4

2–3 medium courgettes, cut in 1.25cm (½in) slices
1–2 tomatoes, quartered
1 large onion, sliced thinly
1 × 2.5ml tsp (½tsp) oregano

Pinch of garlic salt
1 × 2.5ml tsp (½tsp) pepper
1 × 2.5ml tsp (½tsp) grated Parmesan cheese
150g (½oz) butter or bacon fat

Layer courgettes, tomatoes and onion in a dish. Sprinkle with oregano, garlic salt and pepper. Add melted butter or bacon fat and cover with clingfilm. Cook on HIGH for 6–8 minutes. Top with cheese. Cover and let stand for several minutes until cheese melts.

Potato and Mushroom Layer
Nutritious and delicious

Serves 4 to 6

3–4 medium potatoes, cooked and
 sliced
25g (1oz) butter
225g (½lb) fresh mushrooms,
 sliced
2 × 15ml tbsp (2tbsp) wholewheat
 flour
225ml (8fl oz) buttermilk or milk
2 × 2.5ml tsp (2tsp)
 Worcestershire sauce
75g (3oz) mature Cheddar cheese,
 grated
1 × 5ml tsp (1tsp) salt
1 × 2.5ml tsp (½tsp) pepper
 (white preferred)

2 × 15ml tbsp (2tbsp) toasted
sesame seeds (microwave 3–4
minutes, stirring several times)

Microwave potatoes and let stand while preparing other ingredients. Sauté mushrooms in butter 3–4 minutes on HIGH. Add
flour, stirring to blend. Add milk and cook until thickened (3–4
minutes). Remove from microwave and add Worcestershire sauce,
grated cheese, salt and pepper. Peel and layer one half of the
potatoes in a greased casserole. Spoon half the cheese sauce over
potatoes. Layer the remaining potatoes and cheese and top with
sesame seeds. Cook on 80% power until heated throughout.

Baked Spanish Onions

Cut onion in half and top each with pat of butter and ½ beef stock
cube. Add salt and pepper. Cover and cook 1½–2½ minutes per
onion, depending on size. Baste at least once during cooking.

🍴 If using mushrooms to make shish kebabs, cook in microwave
until slightly limp to prevent breakage on skewer.

Cauliflower au Gratin

Serves 6 to 8

1 medium head cauliflower (about
  450g/1lb)
25g (1oz) butter
2 × 15ml tbsp (2tbsp) flour
Pinch of dry mustard

Salt and pepper to taste
225ml (8fl oz) milk
75g (3oz) mature Cheddar cheese,
  grated

Remove outer leaves from cauliflower and trim stem close to base.
Wash and place cauliflower on a plate. Cover with clingfilm and
microwave on HIGH 6–8 minutes. Let stand while making cheese
sauce. Melt butter 1 minute on HIGH. Blend in flour and
seasonings. Stir in milk and microwave on HIGH 2–3 minutes, or
until thickened, stirring every minute. Add cheese and stir to
blend. Place cauliflower on serving plate and pour sauce on top.
Serve at once.

Quick Home-style Baked Beans

Serves 6

2 × 452g (16oz) cans baked beans
  with pork sausages
50ml (2fl oz) ketchup
50g (2oz) brown sugar
1 medium-sized onion, minced or
  2 × 15ml tbsp (2tbsp) onion
  flakes

2 × 5ml tsp (2tsp) prepared
  mustard
2 × 5ml tsp (2tsp) Worcestershire
  sauce
1 × 2.5ml tsp (½tsp) garlic salt
4 slices bacon

Cook bacon 4–5 minutes while gathering remaining ingredients
together. Remove bacon from fat and add onions. Cover and cook
1½–2 minutes on HIGH. Add remaining ingredients, stirring to
blend. Save bacon and crumble, adding to beans at end of cooking
time. Microwave on HIGH for 3–4 minutes. Stir. Reduce power to
50% and microwave for 16–18 minutes. Allow to stand covered
for 5 minutes before serving. (If a moist mixture is desired, leave
covered during entire cooking time.)

🐷 Frozen vegetables don't need extra water and may be cooked
in their own plastic bags. Cut an inch slice on top of bag. Add pat
of butter and cook recommended time.

Potatoes

General rules of thumb for successful potato baking are:

Prick well-scrubbed potatoes and arrange at least 2.5cm (1in) apart on a paper towel so moisture will be absorbed as potatoes cook.

Select potatoes that are uniform in size.

Use this chart as a guide for cooking potatoes:

1 med.	3–5 minutes
2 med.	5–7½ minutes
3 med.	7–10 minutes
4 med.	10½–12½ minutes

Allow sufficient standing time. Wrap potatoes in heavy kitchen towel or foil and allow to stand 5–10 minutes after cooking so potatoes will soften. If a potato is microwaved until it feels soft it has been overcooked and will show signs of dehydration (shrivelling) upon standing.

It is very hard to give specific times for potatoes because of variations in size, maturity, moisture content, type and quality. Check each potato after minimum microwaving time to see if it is beginning to feel soft. If so remove from oven, wrap and let stand as described above.

Stuffed Baked Potatoes
A good dish to prepare ahead

Serves 4
2 large baking potatoes
50g (2oz) Parmesan cheese
3 × 15ml tbsp (3tbsp) single
   cream, or sour cream
25g (1oz) butter
Salt
White pepper

Microwave potatoes according to general rules for baked potatoes (see above). Slice potatoes in half, lengthwise, and remove centre, leaving a 6mm (¼in) thick shell. Whip scooped out potatoes in food processor or mixer and add remaining ingredients. Stuff shells with potato mixture. Arrange in circle on serving plate and microwave on HIGH for 3–5 minutes until hot. Garnish with a dollop of sour cream and sprinkle with chives or paprika.

Quickie Patio Potatoes

Serves 6 to 8

4 potatoes (about 675g/1½lb), thinly sliced
1 packet dry onion soup mix

40g (1½oz) butter
1 × 2.5ml tsp (½tsp) rosemary

Melt butter for 40 seconds on HIGH. Add rosemary. Layer potatoes in casserole dish and sprinkle soup mix over slices. Pour butter over slices. Cover tightly and cook on HIGH 10 minutes. Stir and continue cooking on HIGH until fork tender (about 5–10 minutes).

Sweet Potato Casserole with Crunchy Topping

Serves 6 to 8

3 medium-sized sweet potatoes
2 eggs
50ml (2fl oz) single cream, or evaporated milk
1 × 5ml tsp (1tsp) vanilla
150g (6oz) sugar
1 × 2.5ml tsp (½tsp) salt
25g (1oz) butter

Topping:
75g (3oz) butter
150g (6oz) brown sugar
50g (2oz) flour
100g (4oz) nuts (pecans or walnuts)

Cook 3 medium potatoes in microwave for 10–12 minutes. Wrap in foil for 5–10 minutes to soften. Place potatoes, eggs, milk, vanilla, sugar, salt and butter in food processor or mixer and blend well. Pour in buttered baking dish and microwave on HIGH 10–12 minutes, stirring once.

For topping cut butter into sugar and flour, adding nuts last. Place on top of sweet potatoes and microwave 5–7 additional minutes on 80% power.

Boiled Whole New Potatoes

Serves 4 to 5

6–8 small, whole new potatoes,   150ml (6fl oz) water
  scrubbed

Cover with clingfilm and microwave for 6–8 minutes on HIGH until water boils. Reduce power to 50% and cook for 10–12 minutes until fork tender. Let stand 5 minutes before serving. Season as desired.

Gourmet Potatoes
A good 'do ahead' dish that needs warming only at the last minute

Serves 6 to 8

6 medium-sized potatoes
225g (8oz) shredded Cheddar
  cheese
100g (4oz) butter
225ml (8fl oz) sour cream
4 spring onions, chopped
1 × 5ml tsp (1tsp) salt
Paprika

1 × 2.5ml tsp (½tsp) pepper
(white preferred)

Cook unpeeled potatoes for 18–20 minutes on HIGH. Cool slightly and slice. Melt butter and add cheese, stirring to blend. Add sour cream, salt, pepper and onions. Pour into 20cm × 30cm (8 × 12in) glass baking dish with the potatoes and cook uncovered for 6–8 minutes on HIGH. Saves one hour over conventional cooking.

Supreme Rice Casserole
Great to serve with roast beef

Serves 6

100g (4oz) butter, cut in chunks
225g (8oz) uncooked easy-cook
  rice
1 × 295g (10.4oz) can onion soup

125g (5oz) fresh mushrooms
  sliced, or 1 × 100g (4oz) can
1 × 2.5ml tsp (½tsp) pepper

Combine all ingredients in baking dish. Cover tightly and microwave 5 minutes on HIGH. Stir and microwave 5 additional minutes on 50% power. Let stand several minutes before serving. Simply Scrumptious!

Rice Pilaf

Serves 6 to 8

150g (6oz) long-grain rice
   (preferably Uncle Ben's)
150g (6oz) pearl barley
50g (2oz) butter
8 spring onions, chopped

3 beef stock cubes
850ml (1½pt) boiling water
1 × 100g (4oz) can mushrooms
   with liquid
2 large garlic cloves, optional

Sauté rice and barley in butter 2–3 minutes. Add remaining ingredients and cover tightly. Cook on HIGH for 4–5 minutes and 16–18 minutes on 50% power.

Rice Valencia

Serves 6 to 8

1 chopped onion
½ chopped green pepper
50g (2oz) fresh mushrooms, sliced
2 garlic cloves, crushed
100g (4oz) butter
1 × 2.5ml tsp (½tsp) paprika

250g (9oz) long grain rice
   (preferably Uncle Ben's)
500ml (1pt) chicken stock
100g (4oz) green peas
1 × 5ml tsp (1tsp) salt
2 × 15ml tbsp (2tbsp) chopped red
   pepper

Cover tightly and microwave chopped onions, pepper, mushrooms and garlic cloves in 25g (1oz) butter for 2–3 minutes on HIGH. Add paprika and rice along with chicken stock. Cook for 10 minutes on HIGH and 20–25 minutes on 50% power in a tightly covered container. Remove from oven and add remaining butter, red pepper, green peas and seasonings. Let stand 5 minutes and fluff rice lightly with fork.

Brandied Peaches

2 × 566g (1lb 13oz) cans peach
   halves
225g (8oz) granulated sugar

100ml (4fl oz) brandy, preferably
   peach
Dash of almond essence

Drain peaches, saving 225ml (8fl oz) juice. Set aside. Add sugar to peach juice and cook for 4–5 minutes on HIGH until heavy syrup is formed. Add brandy and almond essence. Pour over peaches and serve warm.

Fruit Compôte

Serves 6

1 can pineapple chunks
1 can apricots
1 can peaches
1 can black cherries

100g (4oz) brown sugar
100g (4oz) butter
1 × 2.5ml tsp (½tsp) cinnamon
1 × 15ml tbsp (1tbsp) cornflour

Flavour to taste with brandy, rum, or sherry – spirit or flavouring. (Use the one of your choice.)

Drain fruit, reserving syrup, and combine in baking dish. Make sauce by combining 100ml (4fl oz) pineapple syrup, apricot syrup, 100ml (4fl oz) syrup from peaches, along with brown sugar and butter. Microwave for 5–6 minutes on HIGH, stirring to dissolve sugar. Mix cornflour with 100ml (4fl oz) liquid from drained fruit and add to fruit to thicken. Add cinnamon and spirits or flavouring. Pour over fruit and microwave for 10–15 minutes on HIGH.

Fruit Medley

Serves 6 to 8

1 small can stoned prunes, drained
1 × 560g (20oz) can pineapple
   chunks, drained
1 × 450g (16oz) can apricot
halves,
   drained

1 × 450g (16oz) can pear halves
   (optional)
½ jar orange marmalade
50–100ml (2–4fl oz) fruit
   flavoured liqueur

Combine all fruit in dish. Pour liqueur and marmalade over mixture. Microwave for 8–10 minutes on 80% power.

Curried Fruit
Deliciously different

Serves 10 to 12

1 can pear halves
1 can apricot halves
1 can peach halves
2 cans pineapple chunks

1 can dark, sweet cherries
75g (3oz) butter
150g (6oz) light brown sugar
2–3 × 5ml tsp (2–3tsp) curry powder

Drain fruit well. Melt butter for 2 minutes. Add sugar and curry powder, stirring to blend. Place fruit in heatproof serving dish. Pour butter mixture over fruit and microwave 12–15 minutes on HIGH.

Glazed Apple Slices

Serves 4

4 large firm apples
225g (8oz) sugar
100g (4oz) butter

2 × 15ml tbsp (2tbsp) lemon juice
1 piece of stick cinnamon, if desired

Wash and core apples. Cut into slices of uniform size. Place sugar, butter, lemon juice and cinnamon stick into a dish and cook on HIGH for 1½ minutes. Add apples and stir to coat. Cover with clingfilm and microwave for 6–7 minutes on HIGH, stirring once. Cook for 6–8 additional minutes at 50% power, until fork tender.

Blushing Peaches

Serves 4 to 5

1 × 566g (1lb 13oz) can peach halves
4 × 15ml tbsp (4tbsp) lemon juice

1 × 2.5ml tsp (½tsp) grated lemon peel
100ml (4fl oz) redcurrant jelly

Drain peach halves and reserve 100ml (4fl oz) of syrup. Place syrup, jelly and lemon juice in a measuring jug. Cook for 6–8 minutes on HIGH until mixture begins to thicken. Pour juice over peaches in serving dish and serve warm.

Pineapple Soufflé

Serves 4 to 5

3 eggs
1 can crushed pineapple
50g (2oz) sugar
2 × 15ml tbsp (2tbsp) flour

25g (1oz) butter
1 × 15ml tbsp (1tbsp)
lemon juice
Salt

Place eggs in a bowl and beat until light. Melt butter for 45 seconds on HIGH. Add butter to eggs, along with remaining ingredients. Cook for 5 minutes on HIGH until mixture starts to thicken. Pour into 1 litre (1¾pt) soufflé dish and finish cooking for 5–8 minutes on 70% power. Delicious served with ham.

Basic Medium White Sauce

Makes 225ml (8fl oz)

25g (1oz) butter
25g (1oz) flour
Salt

White pepper
225ml (8fl oz) milk

Microwave butter on HIGH for 30–40 seconds in a measuring jug or container. Stir in flour, blending to make a smooth, thin paste. Add milk, gradually stirring until smooth. Cook on HIGH 2–3 minutes, stirring every 30 seconds until sauce starts to boil. Sauce will thicken more during standing time.

VARIATIONS:

Thin White Sauce: Use 15g (½oz) each butter and flour and proceed as directed in Basic Medium White Sauce recipe.

Thick White Sauce: Increase butter and flour to 40g (1½oz) each and proceed as directed in Basic Medium White Sauce recipe.

Cheese Sauce: Add to Basic Medium White Sauce recipe 1 × 2.5ml tsp (½tsp) dry mustard, 1 × 5ml tsp (1tsp) Worcestershire sauce and 100g (4oz) grated mature Cheddar cheese. Delicious over cauliflower, broccoli, or asparagus. Also good in casseroles.

🍐 Quick cheese sauce for vegetables: Place processed cheese in measuring jug and heat for 1 minute on 80% power. Stir, and when soft enough, pour over vegetables.

Apple Sauce

Serves 6

4–5 medium cooking apples,
  peeled, cored and sliced
100ml (4fl oz) water

150g (6oz) sugar
1 × 2.5ml tsp (½tsp) cinnamon,
  optional

Place apples and water in casserole and cover with clingfilm.
Microwave on HIGH 9–11 minutes, or until tender. Stir after 5
minutes.

Add sugar and cinnamon to apples and mash with fork, or put
in food processor for a finer texture.

Hollandaise Sauce

2 egg yolks
100g (4oz) butter
Salt

1 × 15ml tbsp (1tbsp) lemon juice
White pepper

Microwave butter in a glass measuring jug for 1 minute on HIGH.
Stir in egg yolks, lemon juice, salt and white pepper, blending well
with wire whisk. Microwave on 70% power for 1–2 minutes,
stirring every 30 seconds. Beat with a wire whisk until smooth.

Horseradish Hollandaise Sauce: Add prepared horseradish to
taste. Fold 100ml (4fl oz) whipped cream into 225ml (8fl oz)
Hollandaise Sauce. Good over vegetables, poached eggs or fish.

Mustard – Cheese Sauce
Delicious on broccoli, Brussels sprouts and cauliflower

75ml (3fl oz) mayonnaise
1 × 2.5ml tsp (½tsp) mustard
Cheddar cheese, grated

1 × 15ml tbsp (1tbsp) dried
  minced onion
1 × 15ml tbsp (1tbsp) lemon juice

Mix above ingredients together and spread on top of cooked
vegetables. Sprinkle with grated Cheddar cheese and place in
microwave. Cook on HIGH for 1 minute.

Simply Scrumptious
Eggs and Cheese

General Guidelines

The egg is cooked even better in the microwave. A simple egg can be turned into so many delicious dishes for the microwave cook. The egg can be used as a breakfast food, brunch item or a main dish.

However, eggs require special cooking techniques when cooked in the microwave:

Many recipes call for egg dishes to be covered with a lid, cover, clingfilm or greaseproof paper to encourage more even cooking.

Eggs usually cook on 70% power.

The yolk of the egg cooks faster than the white due to the higher fat content of the yolk. When poaching an egg, remove the egg from the oven before the white is completely set or the poached egg will be tough.

NEVER cook an egg in the shell. The egg will burst. Eggs can be hard-boiled but not in the shell (see recipe page 64).

The high fat content of cheese attracts microwave energy. Add cheese to casseroles at the end of cooking. Different varieties of cheese vary in hardness, fat, moisture content and in the way they melt. Processed cheeses melt more smoothly than dry, hard, natural cheeses.

If a conventional sauce recipe calls for diced cheese, substitute shredded cheese when converting to microwave cookery. Chunks attract too much microwave energy and require excessive stirring.

Because of its high fat content, cheese melts rapidly and can become tough or stringy when overcooked. When cheese is combined with eggs, cream or milk, use a lower heat control setting to produce a smooth and creamy dish without excessive stirring.

Sauces, creamy quiches and puffy omelettes are just a few of the egg and cheese dishes you can prepare in your microwave. Eggs can be attractive, nutritious and prepared so easily by using the microwave.

Hard-boiled Eggs

Never cook eggs in their shell in the microwave – they will burst. When you need hard-boiled eggs, they can be cooked in the microwave but not in the shell. Eggs cooked this way are perfect for salads, casseroles, garnishes or sandwich fillings.

To hard-boil eggs in the microwave, separate 3 eggs and place in 2 lightly buttered bowls. Stir the yolks with a fork. Cover each bowl with clingfilm. Cook on 50% power. Cook the yolks 45 seconds to 1¼ minutes and cook the whites 2 to 2½ minutes. Remove when slightly underdone. Let stand, covered, for 2 to 3 minutes.

🐦 Reheating egg dishes after original cooking can cause the eggs to toughen.

🐦 Always use the tip of a knife or a wooden cocktail stick to break the egg yolk before cooking.

Poached Eggs Newburg

Serves 6

3 muffins, split and toasted   6 poached eggs

Shrimp-Newburg Sauce:

225ml (8fl oz) Basic White Sauce   Dash paprika
  (see page 00)   1 × 141g (5oz) can shrimps,
2 egg yolks, slightly beaten   drained or 1 × 141g (5oz) can
2 × 15ml tbsp (2tbsp) sherry   crabmeat
Salt

Prepare basic white sauce and slowly add to egg yolks, stirring constantly. Add sherry, salt, paprika and shrimps (or crab). Blend well, and microwave on 70% power 1–2 minutes.

Poach eggs following directions on page 00. Place well-drained poached eggs on toasted muffins and spoon on Shrimp-Newburg sauce. If warmer serving temperature is desired, microwave assembled muffins on 70% power until heated.

Family Breakfast Special

Serves 6 to 8

450g (1lb) sausagemeat
1 × 113g (4oz) can sliced
  mushrooms, drained
Herbed croûtons (see page 118)
150g (6oz) strong cheese, grated
4 eggs
1 × 364g (13oz) can evaporated   1 × 295g (10.4oz) can condensed
  milk   cream of mushroom soup

Microwave the sausagemeat on HIGH for 8 to 12 minutes or until done. Drain sausagemeat and mushrooms in a colander. Place croûtons in a round casserole dish. Layer cheese over croutons, then mushrooms, then sausagemeat. Beat eggs and then add milk and soup to egg mixture. Pour the egg mixture over the layered ingredients. Let stand in the refrigerator overnight. To cook, place a glass (bottom side down) in the centre of the round casserole dish. Cover with clingfilm. Microwave on 70% power for 20 to 30 minutes. Let stand 5 minutes. Parsley can be used as a garnish and a filling at the centre of the dish.

Puffy Omelette
An omelette can be used with any meal –
breakfast, lunch, or supper

Serves 4 to 6
6 eggs, separated
125ml (5fl oz) mayonnaise
50ml (2fl oz) water
40g (1½oz) butter
75g (3oz) Cheddar cheese, grated
1 × 5ml tsp (1tsp) chives, chopped

In one bowl beat egg yolks, mayonnaise and water. Set aside. In another bowl, beat egg whites until peaks form. Gently pour egg yolk mixture over egg whites and gently fold together. In a pie dish melt the butter on HIGH for 45 seconds to 1 minute. Swirl butter to cover the pie dish. Pour the egg mixture into the dish. Cook on 70% power for 6 to 8 minutes, or until the eggs are soft, moist and glossy on top. Sprinkle the cheese and chives over the top of the omelette. Microwave on 70% power for 1 minute or until the cheese starts to melt. With a spatula, loosen around the edge of the omelette. Add topping if desired. Fold the omelette in half and gently slide onto a plate.

Scrumptious Potato Omelette
with Bacon
A tasty treat. Cook and serve in the same dish.

Serves 2 to 3

2 slices bacon
1 medium potato, cooked and
  diced
3 spring onions, sliced
1 × 15ml tbsp (1tbsp) red pepper

1 × 2.5ml tsp (½tsp) salt
2 eggs, well beaten
Dash of pepper
1 × 15ml tbsp (1tbsp) parsley,
  chopped

Cook bacon on HIGH 2 to 3 minutes or until crisp. Drain bacon. Place onions and potato in pie dish and cook on HIGH 2 to 3 minutes. Add eggs, chopped bacon, red pepper, salt and pepper. Microwave on 70% power 2 to 3 minutes, or until eggs are soft and moist. Garnish with chopped parsley.

Scrambled Eggs

Eggs scrambled in a microwave are even better than scrambled eggs cooked conventionally. The eggs will be fluffier and have more volume than conventionally cooked eggs. You can microwave and serve them in the same dish.

To scramble eggs in the microwave:
1. Place butter in a suitable dish. Microwave on HIGH for 30 seconds or until butter melts.
2. Add milk and eggs. Stir well with a fork or wire whisk. Microwave on HIGH for half the cooking time.
3. Stir eggs well. Eggs around the edge of the dish are beginning to set. Stir and move eggs on the outside to the centre of the dish. Microwave on HIGH the remaining time. (If cooking 4 or more eggs, stir once or twice more.)
4. Remove eggs while they are still soft and moist. Let stand 1 to 4 minutes. Stir eggs before serving.

Timetable for Scrambled Eggs
Cook: HIGH Power

Eggs	Butter	Milk	Time
1	1 × 15ml tbsp (1tbsp)	1 × 15ml tbsp (1tbsp)	35–45 seconds
2	1 × 15ml tbsp (1tbsp)	2 × 15ml tbsp (2tbsp)	1¼–1¾ minutes
4	1 × 15ml tbsp (1tbsp)	3 × 15ml tbsp (3tbsp)	2–3 minutes
6	2 × 15ml tbsp (2tbsp)	50ml (2fl oz)	3¼–4½ minutes

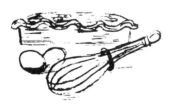

Various fillings can be used to make an omelette an any-meal dish. The plain omelette can be served at breakfast, a fruit-filled omelette makes a nice lunch and a meat-filled omelette makes a delicious and nutritious supper dish.

Brunch Eggs
A nice selection for a brunch

Serves 6 to 8

4 slices buttered toasted bread,
  cubed
4 eggs, beaten
225ml (8fl oz) milk
Dash of Worcestershire sauce

1 × 2.5ml tsp (½tsp) salt
280g (10oz) Cheddar cheese,
  grated
225g (8oz) cooked meat (ham,
  chicken or shrimps)

Combine all ingredients in mixing bowl and stir lightly until all ingredients are mixed together. Pour into a greased 22.5cm (9in) round glass baking dish and cover. Refrigerate overnight or 12 hours. Microwave on 70% power 20 to 25 minutes until centre is set. Let stand 5 minutes before serving.

Poached Eggs

Remember 4 important steps:
1. Bring water and vinegar to a full boil on HIGH. (Vinegar helps egg white to set.)
2. Reduce power to 50% so egg will cook gently.
3. Standing time is important. (Egg white sets without yolk overcooking.) Shake cups gently once or twice during standing time. Do not remove clingfilm.
4. Use a slotted spoon to drain egg.

To poach eggs in the microwave:
1. Measure 2 × 15ml tbsp (2tbsp) water and ¼tsp vinegar into cup. Use one cup per egg. Cover cup with clingfilm. Microwave on HIGH 30 to 45 seconds or until water boils.
2. Break egg into cup. Barely prick yolk with wooden cocktail stick. Cover. Microwave on 50% power 45 seconds to 1 minute 15 seconds or until most of the white is opaque but not set.
3. Let egg stand 2 to 3 minutes or until egg white is set. Shake egg gently once during standing time. Then remove cover.
4. Use a slotted spoon to remove egg. Let drain and then serve.

Timetable for Poached Eggs
Cook: 50% Power

1 egg	*45 seconds to 1 minute 15 seconds*
2 eggs	*1 minute 10 seconds to 1 minute 30 seconds*
4 eggs	*2 minutes 10 seconds to 3 minutes 10 seconds*
6 eggs	*3 minutes 30 seconds to 4 minutes 10 seconds*

Fried Eggs

Eggs can be fried in the microwave in a browning dish. They are quick and delicious:

1. Preheat browning dish on HIGH for 2 to 4 minutes. Place 2 strips of bacon in browning dish. Microwave on HIGH 2 to 3 minutes or until bacon is crisp. Remove and drain.
2. Add 2 eggs to dish. Baste with bacon fat. Microwave on HIGH 1–1½ minutes. Let eggs stand 2 to 3 minutes or until set.

Macaroni Cheese
Children love this

100g (4oz) macaroni, uncooked	100ml (4fl oz) milk
225g (½lb) strong cheese, grated	1 × 2.5ml tsp (½tsp) salt
3 eggs	1 × 2.5ml tsp (½tsp) black pepper
1 × 149g (5.3oz) can evaporated milk	50g (2oz) butter

Cook macaroni conventionally while preparing other ingredients. Grate cheese and blend eggs with milk, salt and pepper. Layer macaroni in 22.5cm (9in) casserole dish alternating with cheese. Pour milk and egg mixture on top. Dot with butter. Microwave on HIGH for 5 minutes. Stir. Cook on 70% power 10 to 12 minutes – stirring once.

This dish is better if made the day before serving. The macaroni may absorb the milk. If the macaroni dish appears dry upon removing from refrigerator, add 50ml (2fl oz) milk before cooking. This dish can be browned conventionally if desired.

Fresh Corn and Cheese Quiche
One of the best quiches you will ever eat!

Serves 6 to 8

6 slices bacon
3 ears fresh corn
3 eggs
150ml (6fl oz) single cream or
  evaporated milk
100g (4oz) Cheddar cheese

2 × 15ml tbsp (2tbsp) green
  pepper
1 × 5ml tsp (1tsp) salt
Pepper, white preferred
1 baked 22.5cm (9in) pastry case*
Paprika
Parsley

Cook bacon on HIGH 5 to 7 minutes or until crisp. Drain and crumble. Cut corn off the cob and set aside. Beat eggs in a glass bowl. Add milk or cream, cheese, green pepper, salt and pepper. Microwave on 70% power for 3 to 4 minutes or until heated thoroughly. Stir well and add corn and bacon. Pour egg and corn mixture into the baked pastry case. Microwave on 70% power for 13 to 17 minutes or until firm around edges. Centre should be slightly soft. Let stand 5 minutes. Sprinkle paprika on top and garnish with parsley.

*See page 138 for pastry case recipe for microwave.

Hollandaise Sauce
A creamy sauce for fish or vegetables

50g (2oz) butter
1 × 15ml tbsp (1tbsp) lemon juice
2 egg yolks, beaten
2 × 15ml tbsp (2tbsp) single cream

1 × 2.5ml tsp (½tsp) dry mustard
Salt
Dash Tabasco

Melt butter in a glass measuring jug on HIGH for 1 minute. Add lemon juice, egg yolks, cream, mustard, salt and Tabasco. Stir well. Microwave on HIGH 1 minute. Beat with a wire whisk until smooth.

🍳 Vinegar is used in poaching eggs to help set the egg whites.

🍳 A wire whisk is an especially helpful piece of equipment to use when you cook with a microwave. It makes sauces and puddings smooth – lumps will disappear.

Basic White Sauce
Can be measured, mixed and cooked in the same cup

25g (1oz) butter
25g (1oz) flour
Salt

Pepper (preferably white pepper)
Pinch of dry mustard
225ml (8fl oz) milk

Melt butter in measuring jug or glass bowl on HIGH 30 to 45 seconds. Stir in flour and seasonings until smooth. Add milk and stir well. Microwave 1½ to 2 minutes on HIGH. Stir well. Microwave on HIGH an additional 1½ to 2 minutes.

Variation: Cheese Sauce: Add 50g (2oz) grated cheese into White Sauce after it has been microwaved. Stir well and serve.

Artichoke Sauce
Complementary sauce for chicken or veal

½ × 424g (15oz) can artichoke
   hearts, chopped
25g (1oz) butter
25g (1oz) flour
Salt
Pepper

1 × 15ml tbsp (1tsp) chicken stock
   granules
100ml (4fl oz) liquid from
   artichokes
100ml (4fl oz) evaporated milk

Melt butter on HIGH for 30–45 seconds. Stir in flour and seasonings until smooth. Add milk and liquid and microwave on HIGH 3–4 minutes stirring several times. Add artichokes.

Elegant Eggs

Serves 4

4 individual pastry cases, baked
50g (2oz) butter
3 medium tomatoes, diced
4 spring onions and tops

100g (¼lb) mushrooms, sliced
2 × 15ml tbsp (2tbsp) fresh parsley
4 eggs, poached
225ml (8fl oz) Hollandaise Sauce

Poach eggs in microwave. (See page 68.) Melt butter on HIGH 30 seconds. Sauté tomatoes, onions and mushrooms on 70% power for 4–6 minutes. Add parsley and stir well. Fill each pastry case with vegetable mixture. Top with a poached egg. Spoon on Hollandaise Sauce. Garnish with paprika and parsley.

Simply Scrumptious
Fish and Seafood

General Guidelines

Fish is excellent microwaved. Because of its high moisture content, it cooks quickly, retains its natural flavour and can be cooked on HIGH.

Fish is delicate and overcooking, therefore, happens quickly. It is cooked the moment it becomes opaque and the centre flakes easily when lifted with a fork. Do not overcook, which makes it dry and chewy.

The internal temperature rises about 5°C (10°F) during standing time. Always let stand 5 minutes before serving.

Completely thaw fish before cooking.

Arrange pieces with thicker parts towards outside of dish.

Cover the dish unless the fish itself is covered with a sauce or coating. Cook uncovered when using coatings to prevent coatings from becoming soggy, and when using sauces to prevent the sauce from becoming watery.

Quick Shrimp Curry

Serves 4

50g (2oz) butter	2 × 5ml tsp (2tsp) curry powder
1 small chopped onion	1 × 2.5ml tsp (½tsp) salt
2–3 × 15ml tbsp (2–3tbsp) chopped green pepper	Dash of pepper
	1 × 2.5ml tsp (½tsp) ginger
2 cloves garlic, crushed	Dash chilli powder
400ml (16fl oz) sour cream	450g (1lb) cooked shrimps
2 × 5ml tsp (2tsp) lemon juice	

Microwave butter, onion, pepper and garlic on HIGH 2–3 minutes. Stir in sour cream, lemon juice, seasonings and spices. Add shrimps. Heat on HIGH 3–4 minutes to serving temperature. Serve over rice with desired condiments.

Cooking Shrimps: Place 450g (1lb) of headless shrimps in their shells in a shallow dish. Add 100ml (4fl oz) water and a dash salt. (Also add bay leaf, lemon slices or pickling spices if desired.) Cover tightly with clingfilm. Cook on HIGH 5–6 minutes, stirring once. Drain and rinse in cold water to stop cooking. For peeled shrimps follow same procedure, but microwave on HIGH 4–5 minutes.

Poached and Steamed Fish

Microwave-poached and microwave-steamed fish is tender and moist because of lack of dry heat. Poaching and steaming produce superior results. Conventionally, fish is poached in a liquid, which flavours the fish and keeps it moist. When converting a conventional recipe to microwave, reduce the liquid. Water, white wine or chicken stock may be used.

Conventional directions call for wrapping a whole fish in cheesecloth to keep it moist and to hold the fish together when it is turned; this is not needed in microwaving. Only a covering on the dish is needed. Cover, allowing a steam vent, and microwave on HIGH 8–11 minutes per 450g (1lb) for whole fish, 5–7 minutes per 450g (1lb) for thick fish steaks, and 2–6 minutes per 450g (1lb) for thinner cuts. When converting steamed fish recipes to microwave, no liquid needs to be added. The moisture content of the fish is sufficient. Just cover with clingfilm and follow the same microwaving times as for poached fish.

Fish Fillets with Caper Butter Sauce

Serves 4
450g (1lb) fish fillets (sole, turbot,
  flounder, haddock or perch)
40g (1½oz) butter

Microwave butter on HIGH about 30 seconds to melt. Coat fish with butter and arrange fish with thickest portions to the outside of the dish. Cover with clingfilm and cook on HIGH 5–7 minutes, or until fish flakes easily. Let rest about 2 minutes while you prepare the sauce.

Caper Butter Sauce:

50g (2oz) butter
2 × 15ml tbsp (2tbsp) parsley,
  chopped
2 × 15ml tbsp (2tbsp) capers,
  crushed

1 × 5ml tsp (1tsp) lemon juice
1 × 2.5ml tsp (½tsp) salt
Dash pepper (preferably white)

Mix sauce ingredients and microwave on HIGH 1–1½ minutes. Drain cooking liquid from fish, pour sauce over and serve.

Other Sauces good with Fish

Almond Butter: Combine 25g (1oz) thinly sliced or slivered almonds with 50g (2oz) butter and microwave on HIGH 2–3 minutes. Spoon over cooked, drained fillets.

Lemon Butter: Combine 2 × 15ml tbsp (2tbsp) lemon juice, 1 × 15ml tbsp (1tbsp) grated lemon peel (optional), 50g (2oz) butter and a dash Tabasco. Microwave on HIGH 1–1½ minutes. Spoon over cooked, drained fillets.

White Wine and Garlic: Combine 50g (2oz) butter, 2 × 15ml

tbsp (2tbsp) white wine, 1 crushed garlic clove, 1 × 2.5ml tsp
(½tsp) salt and dash white pepper. Microwave on HIGH 1–1½
minutes and spoon over cooked, drained fillets.

Herb Butter. Combine 50g (2oz) butter and 2 × 5ml tsp (2tsp)
chopped fresh herbs: dill, chives, basil or parsley. Add a little wine
if desired.

Bacon and Spring Onion: Combine 2 slices cooked bacon, 1 ×
15ml tbsp (1tbsp) chopped spring onion, 1 small tomato, seeded
and chopped, 50g (2oz) butter, 1 × 15ml tbsp (1tbsp) lemon juice,
1 × 2.5ml tsp (½tsp) salt and dash of pepper. Microwave on
HIGH 1–2 minutes. Spoon over cooked, drained fillets.

Baked Scallops

Serves 4

450g (1lb) sea scallops
50g (2oz) butter, melted
2 × 5ml tsp (2tsp) garlic powder

White breadcrumbs
25g (1oz) grated Parmesan cheese

Marinate scallops in butter and garlic for 1 hour or longer.
Microwave in covered dish 3½–5 minutes, stirring once during
cooking to rearrange the scallops. Let stand 1 minute and test
scallops. Texture should be flaky. Cook a little longer if needed.
Sprinkle with breadcrumbs and cheese.

Baked Haddock or Sole

Serves 4

450g (1lb) haddock or sole
Salt and pepper
Grated lemon peel, to taste
2 × 15ml tbsp (2tbsp) lemon juice
2 × 15ml tbsp (2tbsp) chopped
  spring onions

1 × 15ml tbsp (1tbsp) chopped
  parsley
1 × 5ml tsp (1tsp) seasoned salt
100ml (4fl oz) mayonnaise

Arrange fish in baking dish with thickest portions to the outside.
Mix remaining ingredients and spread on fish. Microwave
uncovered on HIGH 5–7 minutes or until done. Garnish with
parsley and lemon peel.

Cold Paella
A favourite summer supper or luncheon dish

Serves 6 to 8

1 × 280g (10oz) packet frozen
  peas
150g (6oz) long-grain rice
500ml (1pt) water
1 jar artichoke hearts

Shrimps, cooked and peeled (about
  450g/1lb)
Spring onions
Small tomatoes or tomato wedges
Beansprouts (optional, if crunch
  desired)

Mix rice and water in a dish. Cover with clingfilm and microwave on HIGH 16–18 minutes, or until done. Let stand covered 10 minutes. Microwave frozen peas on HIGH 2–4 minutes to defrost. Mix all ingredients together except tomatoes and chill. Serve on bed of lettuce with tomatoes on top. Pour over French dressing.

French Dressing:

4 × 15ml tbsp (4tbsp) sugar
1 × 5ml tsp (1tsp) salt
1 × 5ml tsp (1tsp) celery salt
1 × 5ml tsp (1tsp) dry mustard
1 × 15ml tbsp (1tbsp) ketchup

1 onion
3 × 15ml tbsp (3tbsp) vinegar
225ml (8fl oz) oil
1 × 15ml tbsp (1tbsp) lemon juice

Blend all ingredients together in blender.

🐟 Substitute canned salmon for shrimps and brown rice for long-grain rice.

Baked Salmon Steaks

Serves 4

Four 2.5cm (1in) thick salmon
  steaks
25g (1oz) butter
2 × 15ml tbsp (2tbsp) lemon juice

Salt and pepper
1 small onion, sliced
Paprika

Melt butter on HIGH about 30 seconds. Add lemon juice, salt, and pepper. Pour over salmon. Top with onion slices and cook on HIGH 5–6 minutes. Let stand 5 minutes. Serve with lemon wedges.

Sherried Crab

Serves 8 to 10

40g (1½oz) butter
40g (1½oz) flour
400ml (¾pt) milk (or single cream)
1 × 100g (4oz) jar pimento, chopped
¾ green pepper, finely chopped
150g (6oz) tiny green peas (preferably frozen)

1 × 5ml tsp (1tsp) sherry, or to taste
Salt and pepper
2 × 170g (6½oz) cans crabmeat
Grated Parmesan cheese
Paprika

Cook butter and green pepper about 2–3 minutes on HIGH till pepper is soft. Stir in flour. Add milk, pimento and sherry. Microwave about 4–5 minutes on HIGH till mixture starts to boil. Add crab and peas and sprinkle with cheese and paprika. Microwave on HIGH till bubbly, 2–3 minutes. Serve on toast, melba crackers or in pastry cases or vol-au-vents.

Devilled Crab Shells

Serves 6

1 × 170g (6½oz) can white crabmeat
100g (4oz) finely grated breadcrumbs
225ml (8fl oz) mayonnaise
6 hard-boiled eggs, chopped

1 small chopped onion
2 × 15ml tbsp (2tbsp) green olives, sliced
1 × 2.5ml tsp (½tsp) salt
Pinch of garlic powder

Cook onion covered about 30–45 seconds on HIGH. Add all other ingredients. Mix and place in 6 scallop shells or ramekins. Sprinkle with additional breadcrumbs and a small pat of butter on top. Microwave at 70% power 2–4 minutes.

🎄 Whole fish may be baked, steamed or poached, but shielding with foil may be needed on the tail and thin parts to prevent overcooking (if your oven permits use of metal). Cook covered 6–15 minutes per 450g (1lb).

Seafood Medley

Serves 10

225g (8oz) crabmeat
225g (8oz) lobster meat (or
  substitute white chicken meat,
  chopped)
450g (1lb) shrimps, cooked and
  shelled
225ml (8fl oz) mayonnaise
3 × 15ml tbsp (3tbsp) chopped
  green pepper

2 × 15ml tbsp (2tbsp) chopped
  onion
Salt
1 × 5ml tsp (1tsp) Worcestershire
  sauce
100g (4oz) potato crisps
Paprika

Combine all ingredients except crisps and paprika. Spread in casserole dish, cover. Cook on HIGH 5–6 minutes to heat thoroughly, stirring several times. Spread crushed potato crisps over casserole and sprinkle generously with paprika. Microwave uncovered on HIGH 1–2 minutes longer, without stirring.

Gourmet Scampi

Serves 4

325g–450g (12–16oz) peeled
  prawns
1 clove garlic
3 × 15ml tbsp (3tbsp) parsley,
  finely chopped
Paprika

100g (4oz) butter
50ml (2fl oz) dry sherry
2 × 5ml tsp (2tsp) chopped
  shallots
5 × 15ml tbsp (5tbsp) lemon juice
Salt and pepper to taste

Combine all ingredients except prawns and microwave on HIGH 1½–2½ minutes to melt butter and cook thallots. Stir in prawns. Let sit about 10 minutes to blend flavours. Microwave on HIGH 1–2 minutes to serving temperature. Good served with rice.

🔥 Whole lobster or lobster tails can be microwave-steamed in a few minutes. Put 100ml (4fl oz) water in a casserole and microwave on HIGH to boiling. Add lobster, cover and microwave on HIGH till the shell turns red and the meat is white and tender. Overcooking can toughen the meat.

Hot Tuna Salad
Quick supper dish

Serves 6

325g (12oz) sliced potatoes or
450g (1lb) can white potatoes,
drained and sliced
1 × 198g (7oz) can tuna, drained
1 × 15ml tbsp (1tbsp) dried green
pepper
1 stick chopped celery

1 apple, peeled and chopped
1 × 2.5ml tsp (½tsp) dried basil
1 × 15ml tbsp (1tbsp) lemon juice
1 × 2.5ml tsp (½tsp) salt
100ml (4fl oz) French dressing
100ml (4fl oz) fried onion rings

If using fresh potatoes, cook potatoes, apple and celery covered with 100ml (4fl oz) water on HIGH 5–7 minutes, or until tender. If using canned potatoes, cook celery and apple on HIGH about 1–2 minutes. Add all other ingredients except onion rings to potato mixture and microwave on HIGH about 3–5 minutes, until thoroughly heated. Stand 2 minutes and top with onion rings before serving.

Flounder Parmesan

Serves 4

450g (1lb) fillet of flounder
100ml (4fl oz) sour cream
2 × 15ml tbsp (2tbsp) grated
Parmesan cheese
1 × 2.5ml tsp (1tsp) lemon juice

1 × 15ml tbsp (1tbsp) grated
onion
1 × 2.5ml tsp (½tsp) salt
Dash Tabasco
Paprika
Chopped parsley

Cut fish into serving size portions. Arrange fillets in baking dish with thickest portions to the outside. Mix remaining ingredients except paprika and parsley. Spread mixture on fish. Sprinkle with paprika. Cook uncovered on HIGH 5–7 minutes until done. Garnish with parsley.

🐦 Defrosting fish. Fish defrosts very quickly in the microwave. As a rule, allow 2–3 minutes per 450g (1lb) of boneless fish on the defrost setting. Separate the pieces as soon as possible. Remove fish from the oven while it is still a little icy and complete defrosting under cold running water.

Seafood Sauces

Rémoulade Dressing

Makes 500ml (1 pint)

450ml (16fl oz) mayonnaise
1 × 2.5ml tsp (½tsp) chervil
1 × 2.5ml tsp (½tsp) tarragon
1–2 × 15ml tbsp (1–2tbsp)
   chopped spring onion tops
1 × 2.5ml tsp (½tsp) dry mustard
1 × 2.5ml tsp (½tsp) ground red
   pepper
A few drops of Tabasco sauce
2 × 5ml tsp (2tsp) anchovy paste
1 × 5ml tsp (1tsp) chopped sweet
   pickle or relish
2 × 15ml tbsp (2tbsp) prepared
   horseradish
1 × 5ml tsp (1tsp) capers (always
   crush capers for best flavour)
1 × 5ml tsp (1tsp) paprika
1 × 2.5ml tsp (½tsp) cayenne
1 × 2.5ml tsp (½tsp) chopped
   parsley

Combine ingredients and refrigerate. Sauce will keep as long as mayonnaise. Serve over shrimps or crab on a bed of lettuce. (See directions for cooking shrimps on page 73.)

Shrimp Sauce

4 egg yolks
750ml (1½pt) oil
1 × 5ml tsp (1tsp) salt
1 × 2.5ml tsp (½tsp) Tabasco
Juice of 2 lemons
1 × 15ml tbsp (1tbsp) vinegar
1 × 450g (16oz) bottle tomato
   ketchup

Beat egg yolks. In a separate bowl, combine salt, Tabasco, lemon juice and vinegar. Gradually add oil and vinegar mixture to eggs. Mix well and add ketchup. Keeps in refrigerator several weeks.

Cocktail Sauce: 4 × 15ml tbsp (4tbsp) chilli sauce, 2 × 5ml tsp (2tsp) lemon juice, 1 × 5ml tsp (1tsp) Worcestershire sauce, 1 × 5ml tsp (1tsp) grated horseradish, salt and red pepper to taste. Combine ingredients. Good with oysters, shrimps or crab.

Tartare Sauce: 225ml (8fl oz) mayonnaise, 3 × 15ml tbsp (3tbsp) chopped pickle, 1 × 15ml tbsp (1tbsp) chopped parsley, 1 × 15ml tbsp (1tbsp) chopped capers, 2 × 15ml tbsp (2tbsp) chopped stuffed olives, 1 × 5ml tsp (1tsp) chopped onion. Combine ingredients and store in refrigerator.

Simply Scrumptious
Poultry

General Guidelines

Poultry is an all time favourite in the meat category, being economical, low in calories and versatile. When prepared in the microwave it will be very juicy and full of flavour. Listed below are some guidelines to follow when microwaving poultry:

All poultry should be completely thawed before cooking is started. Defrost on 30% power for 6–9 minutes per 450g (1lb). Then let stand 5 minutes, or until the meat feels soft but still cold.

When cooking, choose a large utensil so the cut-up meat does not overlap, and place the larger, thicker pieces to the outside of the dish. After initial cooking, rearrange the pieces so the less cooked parts are on the outside of the utensil. When cooking chicken pieces with a coating or browning agent, do not turn the pieces over. When cooking with a sauce, turn pieces over halfway through cooking.

Turn the whole bird at least once during microwaving; cook the breast side down during the first half of cooking time, turning the breast side up during the last half.

Allow standing time to finish cooking.

Test if the meat is cooked using conventional methods. The legs should rotate and move freely at the joints, meat should be fork tender, with juices clear and showing no pinkish tint.

For best cooking results, select a turkey that weighs no more than 5.5kg–6.3kg (12–14lb). If your oven cavity is small, carefully centre the turkey in the oven, making sure there are 7.5cm (3in) of space between the turkey and oven walls. It is usually necessary to shield the wings and legs with a small piece of foil to prevent overcooking.

For crispy skin, after microwaving place poultry in a 19°C (375°F, Gas Mark 5) oven and cook until skin becomes crisp and brown.

Poussin and chicken pieces microwave so fast that they do not have time to become crisp and brown. Use a browning agent, crumb coating or cook with a sauce.

Whole Turkey

4.5–5kg (10–11lb) turkey

Place turkey, breast side down in a microwave-safe dish. (A bacon or meat rack placed in a casserole dish works well.) Turkey should cook 12 to 15 minutes per 450g (1lb). Divide the cooking time in half. Microwave on HIGH for 10 to 12 minutes. Reduce power to 50% and cook remainder of first half of time. Turn breast side up. Microwave remaining time. Cover turkey with foil and let turkey stand 20 to 25 minutes or until internal temperature reaches 82°C (180°F).

Note: Shield turkey with foil as needed, if permitted in your microwave. Check instruction book.

☘ Be sure the poultry items are thoroughly defrosted before they are cooked in the microwave.

Marinated Turkey

1.2kg (2½lb) boneless turkey roast
1 × 5ml tsp (1tsp) thyme

Pinch cayenne pepper
1 × 15ml tbsp (1tbsp) lemon juice

Mix thyme, cayenne pepper and lemon juice in a large plastic bag. Add turkey roast to bag and secure. Leave overnight. Turn roast several times during marinating. Remove roast from bag and place on a baking rack. Microwave on HIGH 5 minutes. Turn turkey roast over. Continue to cook on 50% power 25 to 35 minutes. Let stand 10 to 20 minutes, covered with foil. (Meatiest portions should reach 82°C (180°F) when tested with a meat thermometer.)

Chicken Cordon Bleu
An elegant chicken dish with ham and cheese

6 medium whole chicken breasts, boned
225g (8oz) cheese slices
225g (8oz) sliced cooked ham
3 × 15ml tbsp (3tbsp) plain flour
1 × 5ml tsp (1tsp) paprika

75g (3oz) butter, melted
100ml (4fl oz) dry white wine
1 chicken stock cube
1 × 15ml tbsp (1tbsp) cornflour
225ml (8fl oz) whipping cream

Place chicken breast between greaseproof paper. Pound to flatten to 6mm (¼in) thickness. Place cheese and ham on chicken. Roll chicken breast over filling and fasten edges with cocktail sticks. Mix flour and paprika on greaseproof paper and coat chicken. Place chicken in dish. Melt butter on HIGH 45 seconds or until melted. Pour butter over chicken. Cook 5 minutes on HIGH. Add wine and stock. Microwave on 70% power for 25–30 minutes or until tender. Blend cornflour and cream and gradually add to chicken. Cook on 70% power for 2 to 3 minutes or until thickened.

🍤 Cook a whole chicken or turkey – or turkey breast – with the breast side down for the first half of the cooking time and then turn breast side up for the remainder of the time.

Chicken Ratatouille
A prize-winning recipe

Serves 4

50ml (2fl oz) oil
2 whole chicken breasts (boned,
    skinned and thinly sliced)
2 small courgettes, thinly sliced
1 small aubergine (peeled and cut
    in 2.5cm/1in cubes)
1 large onion, thinly sliced
1 × 5ml tsp (1tsp) dried parsley
1 medium green pepper (seeded
    and cut in 2.5cm/1in cubes)

225g (½lb) mushrooms, sliced
450g (1lb) tomatoes (peeled and
    cut in wedges)
2 garlic cloves, crushed
1 × 5ml tsp (1tsp) salt
1 × 5ml tsp (1tsp) basil
1 × 2.5ml tsp (½tsp) black pepper

Heat oil in a casserole on 80% power for 2 minutes. Add chicken and sauté on HIGH for 4–6 minutes. Add courgettes, aubergine, onion, green pepper, mushrooms and spices and cover tightly. Microwave on HIGH 5–8 minutes or until chicken is done and vegetables are tender crisp. Add tomatoes and stir gently. Microwave on 50% power 2–3 minutes. Serve with rice.

Chicken Coatings

Coatings can be put on chicken to give an attractive appearance or to enhance the flavour. These recipes will coat 1.2–1.5kg (2½–3lb) of chicken pieces.

Combine all coating ingredients in a shallow dish or on greaseproof paper. Melt butter in a shallow dish. Add eggs and beat well. Dip chicken in egg mixture and then in coating mixture.

Corn Meal Coating:
100g (4oz) corn meal
2 × 15ml tbsp (2tbsp) celery seeds
2 × 15ml tbsp (2tbsp) paprika

Dip:
40g (1½oz) butter
2 eggs

Extra Crisp Coating:
Fried onion rings, crushed

Dip:
15g (½oz) butter
2 eggs
1 × 15ml tbsp (1tbsp) milk

84

Cheese and Crunchy:
75–100g (3–4oz) cornflake crumbs
  or breadcrumbs
25g (1oz) Parmesan cheese
1 × 15ml tbsp (1tbsp) parsley
  flakes
1 × 5ml tsp (1tsp) garlic salt
Dash pepper

Dip:
50g (2oz) butter
2 eggs

Place chicken in dish, placing meaty pieces to outside. Microwave on HIGH 8–10 minutes and reduce to 10% power for 15–18 minutes. Let stand 5 minutes.

Spicy Turkey or Chicken
A great way to use left-over chicken or turkey

50g (2oz) butter
40g (1½oz) flour
225ml (8fl oz) chicken stock
  (home-made is best)
225ml (8fl oz) milk
100ml (4fl oz) mayonnaise
100ml (4fl oz) whipping cream
1 × 2.5ml tsp (½tsp) curry powder
2 × 5ml tsp (2tsp) Worcestershire
  sauce

Make a white sauce by microwaving butter on HIGH for 1 minute or until melted. Stir in flour. Add chicken stock and blend well. Microwave on 70% power 4 to 5 minutes or until thickened. Whip in remaining ingredients.

Pour sauce over:
1 bunch broccoli, cooked and
  divided into florets
25g (1oz) Parmesan cheese, grated

4 servings chicken or turkey,
  cooked and sliced

Heat casserole on 70% power for 6 to 10 minutes or until bubbly. Top with freshly grated Parmesan cheese.

🖐 To help with counting calories, skin the chicken or turkey before cooking.

Chicken Breast Parmesan

1 × 225g (8oz) bottle tomato
  sauce
2 garlic cloves, crushed
2.5ml tsp (½tsp) basil
2.5ml tsp (½tsp) oregano
2.5ml tsp (½tsp) salt
50g (2oz) cornflakes, crushed
25g (1oz) grated Parmesan cheese

2 × 5ml tsp (2tsp) sesame seeds
1 × 5ml tsp (1tsp) chopped parsley
6 large chicken breasts, split and
  skin removed
1 egg, beaten
1 × 5ml tsp (1tsp) water
50g (2oz) Mozzarella cheese

In a small shallow bowl, beat egg and add water. Set aside.
Combine tomato sauce, garlic, basil, oregano and salt in a
measuring jug. Cover with clingfilm and microwave on HIGH for
1½–2½ minutes. Stir and microwave 3–5 minutes at 50% power.
Remove and set aside. Mix cornflake crumbs, Parmesan cheese,
sesame seeds and parsley. Dip chicken in egg mixture and then in
crumbs. Place in 30cm × 20cm (12 × 8in) baking dish. Cook on
HIGH 5–8 minutes. Continue to microwave at 70% power for
10–13 minutes or until chicken is done. Pour tomato sauce
mixture over chicken. Sprinkle Mozzarella cheese over chicken.
Cook on 70% power for 2–4 minutes or until cheese melts.

Hot Turkey Salad
Rich and delicious

675g (1½lb) chopped turkey
  (cooked)
4 sticks chopped celery
225ml (8fl oz) mayonnaise
2 × 15ml tbsp (2tbsp) diced onion
1 × 295g (10.4oz) can condensed
  cream of chicken soup

1 × 100g (4oz) jar pimento
1 × scant 15ml tbsp (1 scant tbsp)
  lemon juice
Salt and pepper to taste

Mix all ingredients together and place in a 32.5 × 22.5 × 5cm (13
× 9 × 2in) dish. Top salad with:

50g (2oz) melted butter

50g (2oz) breadcrumbs

Microwave on 70% power 10 to 12 minutes or until casserole is
hot and bubbly.

Chinese Barbecued Chicken

50ml (2fl oz) soy sauce
1 × 15ml tbsp (1tbsp) vegetable oil
3 × 15ml tbsp (3tbsp) brown sugar
1 × 5ml tsp (1tsp) dry mustard
1 × 2.5ml tsp (½tsp) ground ginger
1 garlic clove, crushed
1.25–1.5kg (2½–3lb) chicken, skin removed

Mix first 6 ingredients in a dish. Add chicken and coat with sauce mixture. Let chicken marinate in sauce for at least 30 minutes. Microwave on HIGH 8 to 10 minutes. Turn chicken over and baste with sauce. Continue to cook 13 to 16 minutes on 70% power or until chicken is tender.

*This recipe works well cooked in microwave and finished under grill.

Chicken à la Fruit
A delicious and colourful chicken dish to please any gourmet!

50g (2oz) butter, melted
2 × 178ml (6¼oz) cans frozen orange juice concentrate
2 garlic cloves, crushed
50ml (2fl oz) ketchup
50ml (2fl oz) lemon juice
2 × 15ml tbsp (2tbsp) soy sauce
1 × 5ml tsp (1tsp) allspice
Pinch of ginger
1 × 2.5ml tsp (½tsp) salt
6 whole chicken breasts, split and skinned
Juice of a whole lemon
2 bananas, peeled and sliced
1 × 311g (11oz) can mandarin orange sections, drained
1 × 75g (3oz) jar maraschino cherries, drained

Mix first 9 ingredients in a small mixing bowl and stir well. Place chicken in a baking dish. Pour orange juice mixture over the chicken and cover. Place in refrigerator and let chicken stand in mixture several hours to overnight. Drain marinade from chicken and reserve. Cook chicken on HIGH 10 minutes. Baste with marinade and continue cooking on 70% power 12–15 minutes or until done. Place bananas in lemon juice and stir well to coat. Drain bananas adding orange sections and cherries. Add fruit mixture to chicken and cook on 70% power 2–3 minutes longer.

Cheesy Chicken

1.25–1.5kg (2½–3lb) chicken,
  cut up
Garlic salt
Paprika
50g (2oz) Parmesan cheese, grated

100g (4oz) seasoned breadcrumbs
2–3 eggs, well beaten
2–3 × 15ml tbsp (2–3tbsp) milk
100g (4oz) butter, melted

Season chicken with paprika and garlic salt. Beat eggs and milk in shallow bowl. Place breadcrumbs and cheese in shallow bowl and blend. Coat chicken first in egg mixture and then in breadcrumb mixture. Place chicken in a dish with meaty portions to outside. Pour butter over chicken and sprinkle over any remaining breadcrumbs. Cover with greaseproof paper and microwave on HIGH 5–8 minutes. Continue to cook on 70% power 15–18 minutes or until done. Let stand 5 minutes.

Chicken in a Wink

Serves 4 to 6
1.5kg (3lb) chicken breast
1 × 295g (10.4oz) can condensed
  cream of mushroom soup
1 × 295g (10.4oz) can condensed
  cream of chicken soup
1 packet dry onion soup mix
100ml (4fl oz) sherry
1 garlic clove, crushed

40g (1½oz) toasted, sliced
  almonds
150ml (6fl oz) sour cream

Place chicken in a dish with the meatiest parts to the outside. Combine the 3 soups, sherry, and garlic in a bowl. Coat chicken with sauce. Cover with clingfilm. Cook 10 to 12 minutes on HIGH. Rearrange less-cooked portions to outside. Cook on 70% power 15 to 18 minutes or until chicken is fork tender. Allow to stand covered 10 minutes. Remove chicken and add sour cream to gravy. Garnish with toasted almonds.

🐓 To test that poultry is cooked: Check meat next to the bone. The meat should be fork tender. The juices should be clear with no hint of pink.

Baked Chicken with Artichokes
One of the tastiest chicken dishes you will ever eat!

100g (¼lb) mushrooms, thinly
  sliced
1 onion, finely chopped
2 garlic cloves, finely chopped
1.5kg (3lb) meaty chicken pieces
25g (1oz) flour
1 × 5ml tsp (1tsp) salt

1 × 5ml tsp (1tsp) paprika
1 × 2.5ml tsp (½tsp) dried
  rosemary
White pepper
100ml (4fl oz) chicken stock
50ml (2fl oz) dry sherry
1 × 150g (6oz) can artichoke
  hearts,
    drained

Mix mushrooms, onion and garlic in a dish. Mix flour, salt, paprika, rosemary and white pepper. Coat chicken in flour mixture. Place chicken on top of vegetables. Pour chicken stock and sherry over chicken and vegetables. Cook on HIGH for 10 minutes. Move chicken pieces on outside of dish to centre and centre pieces to outside. Continue to cook on 70% power 12 to 15 minutes or until chicken is done. Add artichoke hearts and gently stir into chicken dish. Bake on 70% power 3 to 5 minutes. Let stand 5 minutes.

Oriental Chicken

4 chicken breasts
2 × 15ml tbsp (2tbsp) oil
75g (3oz) mangetout peas
50g (2oz) mushrooms, thinly sliced
2 × 15ml tbsp (2tbsp) spring
  onions, thinly sliced
50g (2oz) water chestnuts

225ml (8fl oz) water
1 chicken stock cube
2 × 15ml tbsp (2tbsp) soy sauce
2 × 5ml tsp (2tsp) cornflour
1 × 2.5ml tsp (½tsp) ground
  ginger
Pepper

Skin and bone chicken and cut into bite-sized pieces. Mix chicken and oil in glass casserole. Microwave on HIGH 8 to 10 minutes. Let stand covered 5 minutes. Add peas, mushrooms, spring onions, and water chestnuts. Microwave on HIGH 4 to 5 minutes. Remove from microwave.

In glass bowl place water, chicken stock cube , cornflour, soy sauce and spices. Cook on HIGH 3 minutes or until thickened. Stir every minute. Pour over chicken and stir well. Serve with rice.

Honey and Sesame Chicken
Try this dish!

Serves 4 to 6

100g (4oz) butter
100ml (4fl oz) honey
2 × 15ml tbsp (2tbsp) prepared
  mustard
50ml (2fl oz) lemon juice

1.25–1.5kg (2½–3lb) chicken,
  cut-up
Salt to taste
2 × 15ml tbsp (2tbsp) toasted
  sesame seeds

Melt butter on 70% power for 1 to 1½ minutes. Add honey, lemon juice, and mustard, and stir well. Salt to taste. Place chicken in 32.5cm × 22.5cm × 5cm (13 × 9 × 2in) dish. Meaty portions of chicken should be placed to outside of dish. Pour honey mixture over chicken. Refrigerate several hours. Microwave on HIGH 12 minutes. Rearrange chicken so less cooked portions are to outside of dish. Baste chicken. Microwave on 70% power for 10 to 12 minutes or until chicken is fork tender. Let stand 5 minutes covered. Sprinkle toasted sesame seeds on chicken and serve.

Turkey Breast
Juicy and delicious

2.25–2.75kg (5–6lb) turkey breast

Place a turkey breast, breast side down in a dish, or on a bacon or meat rack placed in a casserole dish. Divide the cooking time in half. Microwave on HIGH for 5 to 8 minutes. Reduce to 50% power and cook remainder of the first half of time. Turn breast side up. Microwave remaining time or until internal temperature is 82°C (180°F). Cover turkey with foil and let turkey stand 10 to 15 minutes.

Note: Total cooking time is 11 to 15 minutes per 450g (1lb).

Tips to test that Turkey is cooked:
1. With a probe, temperature should reach 82°C (180°F). Check temperature several places in the turkey.
2. Juices should run clear with no hint of pink.
3. Legs should move freely.
4. Meat should be done with no hint of pink.

Simply Scrumptious Meats

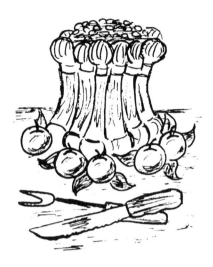

General Guidelines

Successful beef and pork cookery requires a higher level of skill and more attention – whether cooking conventionally or microwaving. Meats cooked in the microwave can be juicy and tender if properly cooked. Meats cooked more than 15–20 minutes brown nicely in their own juices.

You will find that if you select meat wisely, store it properly and choose appropriate cooking methods, microwaved beef and pork will be more full of flavour, tender and juicy than conventionally cooked meat.

Meat Characteristics when Microwaving:

Shape of Roast: Evenly shaped meats cook more evenly. Irregular shapes cook faster in thin areas. Shielding this area with foil (if your oven's instruction manual permits) gives more even cooking.

Bone: Bones conduct heat. When a bone is on one side of a roast, that side cooks first. Boneless cuts of meat cook slower, but more evenly. Bones surrounded by more than 2.5 cm (1 in) of meat have little effect on cooking.

Less Tender Cuts: As in conventional cooking, less tender cuts of meat need moist methods of cooking, while tender cuts must be dry roasted or grilled. In the microwave, cover less tender cuts tightly and reduce the power level to 50% or lower for longer, slower cooking. Use less liquid than you would conventionally since little evaporation takes place. Less tender cuts may be cooked in the microwave crock pot.

Fat: As in conventional cooking, meat with some fat on it is more tender than very lean meat. Even layers of fat on the outside of the meat help it microwave evenly. If the fat cover is heavy on one area, the meat next to it will cook faster and can easily overcook. It may be necessary to trim fat evenly for better results.

Drippings: For more efficient cooking, and to help prevent splatters, remove fat drippings at intervals during cooking because they absorb microwave energy away from lean meat and this slows the cooking process.

Turning or Rotating: Turning of food is more important with larger cuts of meat. Rotating, however, is not necessary in many ovens. Follow manufacturer's directions for this procedure.

Standing Time: This is extremely important since meat continues to cook and tenderise. Do not test that the meat is cooked until after completing the standing time. The internal temperature will rise at least 10–15 degrees during this period. If you decide the meat is not done, it may be microwaved longer after standing. Make a tent of foil, shiny side down, over the meat during standing time to hold in moisture and complete the cooking process. If meat is wrapped tightly, however, it will have a steamed flavour.

Roast Beef in Rock Salt

Rock salt completely encases roast beef, holding in moisture so it does not become tough and dried out. Best cooked to rare or medium.

Serves 8 to 10
2–2.25kg (4–5lb) beef for roasting
  (sirloin or chuck)
6–9 garlic cloves, cut in half
2 sticks of celery, cut in 7.5cm
  (3in) slices
1 medium onion, sliced
2.25kg (5lb) box rock salt
1 large roasting bag
Freshly ground black pepper
Soy sauce

Blot roast well with paper towels. Cut 12 to 14 slits in roast, dividing between all four sides. Place a garlic half in each slit. Rub soy sauce and pepper on roast. Place in roasting bag in a large dish, such as a 3 litre (5pt) casserole. Pour 3.75cm–5cm (1½–2in) of rock salt in bottom of bag. Place celery and onion slices on top of salt. Pour in remainder of salt and pat salt in place, being sure there is 3.75cm–5cm (1½–2in) of salt on all sides. Use a string or rubber band to close the top of the bag. Pull the bag tight so the salt will stay in place. Make 3 slits in top of bag for steam to escape. Microwave for 10 minutes on HIGH, and 45–60 minutes on 30% power. If available, use probe to check temperature, cooking to 55°C (130°F) for rare and 65°C (150°F) for medium. It is best to remove at 55°C (130°F) because the hot rock salt will still continue to cook the meat.

When roast is done, let stand 10 minutes. Scrape salt from roast carefully, because salt will be very hot. Use a vegetable brush to remove remaining salt from roast. It will not have a salty taste if salt is carefully brushed off. Even tougher cuts of meat such as chuck will be tender, moist and delicious.

🍴 Instead of using soy sauce brushed on roast, use Marinade recipe on page 110 for a delicious, flavoured roast.

93

Veal Marsala

Serves 2

225g (½lb) veal, sliced
Salt and pepper to taste
100g (4oz) fresh mushrooms
1 medium sized onion, chopped

100g (4oz) butter
50ml (2fl oz) sherry
100ml (4fl oz) Marsala wine
Chopped parsley

Microwave butter for 45–60 seconds on HIGH until melted. Add veal and sauté on HIGH for 30 seconds. Turn over and cook 30 seconds. Add mushrooms and onion. Sauté covered for 2–3 minutes on HIGH. Add sherry and Marsala and microwave about 2 minutes on HIGH, just to heat. Sprinkle with parsley and serve over rice. Delicious!

Crown Roast of Pork
with Rice Stuffing
A crown roast makes a dramatic party presentation

Serves 8

2.75–3.25kg (6–7lb) crown roast
of pork (Order crown roast from
your butcher several days before
needed. Have the butcher trim
uncut pork ribs and form a
crown, removing backbone for
easy carving.)
1 × 2.5ml tsp (½tsp) rosemary
leaves, crushed
1 × 5ml tsp (1tsp) seasoned salt

Stuffing:
225g (½lb) of your favourite,
seasoned sausage meat
2–3 sticks celery, thinly sliced
225g (½lb) fresh mushrooms,
sliced
1 large onion, chopped
1 × 15ml tbsp (1tbsp) dried
parsley
1 × 2.5ml tsp (½tsp) salt

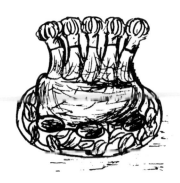

1 × 2.5ml tsp (½tsp) white pepper
325g (12oz) cooked rice
(preferably Uncle Ben's)

Microwave crumbled sausage in a 2 litre (3½pt) casserole on HIGH for 2–3 minutes. Break up with fork and place on paper towel to drain. Place celery, mushrooms and onions in same dish that sausage was in and microwave for 5–6 minutes on HIGH. Stir in sausage along with remaining ingredients. Set aside while preparing roast for microwaving.

Insert meat thermometer (if used) in a meaty area between two ribs, making sure thermometer does not touch bone or fat. Place roast on microwave rack with bony ends down. Rub with rosemary leaves and seasoned salt until dissolved. Cook roast on HIGH for 5–8 minutes.

The following cycle of cooking will be at 50% power for 15–17 minutes per 450g (1lb).

1. Halfway through the final cycle turn roast over with rib end up.
2. Insert meat thermometer (if used) in a meaty area between the ribs, making sure the thermometer does not touch bone or fat, and microwave until about 20 minutes of cooking time remains.
3. Fill roast cavity lightly with rice stuffing, covering **stuffing only** with clingfilm to prevent drying out. Save remaining stuffing to place around roast when served.
4. Cook remaining time, or until the internal temperature reaches 75°C (170°F).
5. Remove from microwave and cover roast loosely with foil. Let stand 10–20 minutes, or until temperature reaches 82°C (180°F).

Transfer roast to serving platter, using a large metal spatula to support stuffing. Garnish rib end with sliced crab apples, pieces of orange or paper frills. To serve carve between chops.

Ham Cookery

The secret to a tender, flavourful ham cooked in the microwave is *slow* cooking – yet cooking time will be half that of conventional cooking!

Type of Ham	Approx min 450g/lb	Start at HIGH POWER	Finish at 40% POWER
Picnic Shoulder (Cook-before-eating kind)	16–18	8 min	70°C (160°F)
Picnic Shoulder (Fully cooked)	16–18	5 min	50°C (130°F)
Bone-in (Cook-before-eating kind)	16–18	8 min	70°C (160°F)
Bone-in (Fully cooked)	12–14	5 min	50°C (130°F)
Canned Ham	6–8	4 min	50°C (130°F)
Boneless rolled ham	6–8	4 min	50°C (130°F)

Tips for Ham Cookery

Place ham on rack to cook. (If rack isn't available, use an inverted saucer on which to place ham.)

If a shield is used it should be at least 2.5cm (1in) from the walls and 7.5cm (3in) from the top of oven.

Remove from oven. Loosely cover with foil and allow to stand 10 minutes. Temperature will rise at least 3°C–5°C (5°F–10°F.)

Ham and Broccoli Bundles with Cheesy Pepper Sauce
Perfect for a luncheon dish

4 thin slices of cooked ham
Prepared mustard

1 × 283g (10oz) packet of frozen broccoli stalks
Cheesy Pepper sauce (see below)

Thaw frozen broccoli stalks 2–3 minutes on 30% power or defrost. Spread ham slices lightly with mustard. Wrap each slice around drained broccoli stalks. Place in greased baking dish. Brush with melted butter. Cover tightly and cook on HIGH 4–5 minutes. While broccoli stands, make cheesy pepper sauce.

Cheesy Pepper Sauce

25g (1oz) flour	225ml (8fl oz) milk
25g (1oz) butter	2 × 15ml tbsp (2tbsp) diced red
Salt	pepper
White pepper	75g (3oz) grated cheese

Make white sauce by melting butter 45 seconds on HIGH. Add flour, salt and pepper and red pepper, stirring to blend. Add milk. Cook for 3–5 minutes on 70% power, stirring several times. After mixture thickens, add cheese, stirring until well blended. Serve hot over ham rolls.

Stir-fry Beef or Pork
A good time to use a food processor!

Serves 4

450g (1lb) minced beef or pork (veal may also be used)	1 small cabbage, shredded
	2 carrots, sliced thinly (diagonally)
3 × 15ml tbsp (3tbsp) soy sauce (or to taste)	1 medium onion, sliced thinly
	2 garlic cloves
3 × 15ml tbsp (3tbsp) sesame seed oil (this adds a special flavour)	Dash of ginger

Microwave minced beef or pork 5–6 minutes on HIGH. Add 1 × 15ml tbsp (1tbsp) each of soy sauce and sesame seed oil. Cover and set aside. Combine cabbage, onion, carrots, garlic, remaining soy sauce and sesame oil. Microwave covered 4–5 minutes until lightly steamed (cabbage should not be soft). Combine vegetables with meat and add a dash of ginger, salt, pepper, additional soy sauce and sesame oil to taste. Delicious served with crusty bread.

For an attractive centrepiece or elegant buffet table, fashion ham to resemble a peacock. Score and stud the ham with cloves. Attach a carved sweet potato for the head, with a ruffle around the neck, olives for eyes, frilled party picks for a crown, and for the tail attach a fan of skewered fruits.

Braised Barbecued Ribs
Ribs are so tender they almost slip from the bone

Serves 4

2kg (4lb) spare ribs, cut in 2–3in pieces

250ml (½pt) barbecue sauce (see recipe below)
1 lemon, thinly sliced

Arrange ribs in bottom of 30cm × 20cm (12 × 8in) dish. Arrange lemon slices over top. Cover tightly with clingfilm. Cook on HIGH 5 minutes. Reduce power to 40% and cook for 20–25 minutes. Drain. Turn ribs over and rearrange so least-cooked ribs are to the outside. Overlap more cooked parts. Add barbecue sauce and re-cover tightly with clingfilm. Microwave 20–25 minutes at 40% power until fork tender.

Barbecue Sauce
Delicious on pork ribs, meat balls and chicken

Makes about 600ml (1¼pt)

1 medium onion, finely chopped
2 garlic cloves, minced
400ml (16fl oz) tomato sauce or ketchup
75g (3oz) brown sugar

50ml (2fl oz) cider vinegar
100ml (4fl oz) water
50ml (2fl oz) Worcestershire sauce
Few drops Tabasco

Place onions and garlic in a container. Cover with clingfilm and cook for 2–3 minutes on HIGH. Add remaining ingredients and cook for 4 minutes on HIGH and 4–6 minutes on 50% power. Store leftover sauce in refrigerator and use on chicken, pork or beef.

Barbecued Spare Ribs

Precook ribs in the microwave and finish up on the grill, saving lots of time without sacrificing that wonderful barbecue flavour.

2kg (4lb) lean spare ribs, cut into individual ribs

Barbecue sauce (see recipe above)

Place ribs on side in large rectangular dish. Cover loosely with greaseproof paper and cook on HIGH 18–20 minutes until fork tender. (Rearrange ribs after cooking first 10 minutes.) Drain and transfer to grill. Cook 10 minutes. Brush with sauce and cook 5 minutes, turning several times.

Minced Pork Patties

Speedy and delicious with an oriental flavour.
Use browning dish

450g (1lb) minced pork   1 chopped tomato
1 medium onion, chopped   3 eggs

Add onion, tomato and eggs to minced pork and form into patties. Preheat browning dish for 8–9 minutes. Cook on HIGH 2 minutes on first side and 2–3 minutes on second side. Add soy sauce to each patty and eat like a hamburger.

Lamb with Herb Mustard Coating

Microwaved lamb gives juicy, tender results

1 × 2.5ml tsp (½tsp) rosemary
1 clove garlic, mashed
1 × 15ml tbsp (1tbsp) soy sauce
4 × 15ml tbsp (4tbsp) Dijon
  mustard
50ml (2fl oz) olive oil or cooking
  oil
A small leg of lamb

Mix rosemary, garlic, soy sauce and mustard in a small bowl. Using a wire whisk, beat in oil a few droplets at a time to make an emulsion.

Place the lamb on a rack in a baking dish, fat side down. If your oven permits the use of foil, shield the end of the leg bone with aluminium foil to cover about 5cm (2in) of meat. This will prevent overcooking.

Spread half the coating on top of the lamb before cooking. If using a temperature probe, insert it into the meat so that it is not touching fat or bone and the tip of the probe is in the centre of a large meat muscle. Microwave at 50% power to 82°C (180°F) for well done.

If you are **not** using a temperature probe, but are cooking by time rather than temperature, allow about 12 minutes per 450g (lb) for well done.

Estimate total cooking time and turn the lamb over about halfway through cooking. Drain the fat from the dish and spread the remaining coating mixture on the lamb after turning.

Continue to drain the fat from the dish as it accumulates during cooking. Turn the dish during cooking, as required by your oven to give even cooking results. Some ovens require more turning than others. Serve with the coating.

Spaghetti Sauce

Serves 6

450g (1lb) minced lean beef	2 × 5ml tsp (2tsp) oregano
225g (½lb) Italian sausage	1 × 2.5ml tsp (½tsp) marjoram
1 × 817g (1lb 13oz) can tomatoes	3 garlic cloves, minced
150g (6oz) tomato purée	1 bay leaf
1 large, thinly sliced onion	2 × 5ml tsp (2tsp) salt
1 piece of pork, such as a ham	1 × 15ml tbsp (1tbsp) sugar
bone or pork chop	1 × 5ml tsp (1tsp) black pepper

Cook minced beef, Italian sausage and onions for 5–8 minutes on HIGH until no longer pink. Stir and drain. Add remaining ingredients and cook for 20 minutes on HIGH. Stir and microwave for 40–50 minutes on 50% power. Taste and adjust seasoning. Cook an additional 30 minutes if you prefer a long-simmered flavour.

🐟 If Italian sausage is not available sauté 1 × 5ml tbsp (1tbsp) fennel seed in 2 × 15ml tbsp (2tbsp) oil on HIGH for 1 minute. Let stand about 5 minutes for flavours to blend and then strain oil into spaghetti sauce. Add 225g (½lb) minced pork or beef instead of sausage. Since fennel is used to flavour Italian sausage it will add the same flavour to the sauce.

Spaghetti Pie

Serves 6 to 8

Crust:

225g (8oz) spaghetti, cooked
25g (1oz) Parmesan cheese

15g (½oz) butter
1 egg, beaten

Filling:

225g (½lb) minced beef
225g (½lb) sausage
1 medium onion, chopped
2–3 garlic cloves, crushed
1 × 424g (15oz) bottle tomato
  sauce
1 × 15ml tbsp (1tbsp) sugar

1 × 2.5ml tsp (½tsp) salt
1 × 2.5ml tsp (½tsp) pepper
1 × 5ml tsp (1tsp) basil
1 × 5ml tsp (1tsp) oregano
225g (8oz) cottage cheese
40g (1½oz) Mozzarella cheese

Mix spaghetti, Parmesan cheese, eggs and butter in large bowl. Turn onto large platter, pressing spaghetti evenly to bottom and sides to form a crust. Cook on HIGH 3–5 minutes. Place beef, sausage, onion and garlic in 2 litre (3½pt) bowl and cook on HIGH for 5–7 minutes. Stir occasionally. Drain off fat. Add tomato sauce and all seasonings. Cook 6–8 minutes on HIGH. Spread cottage cheese over spaghetti crust. Pour tomato and meat mixture over cottage cheese. Cover tightly with clingfilm and cook on HIGH 6–8 minutes until heated thoroughly. Add Mozzarella and serve at once.

Pork Chop Casserole

4 pork chops 1.8cm (¾in thick)
2–3 medium-sized potatoes, sliced
  thinly
1 medium onion, sliced thinly
Pinch of basil and oregano

1 × 298g (10½oz) can condensed
  cream of mushroom soup
50g (2oz) Parmesan cheese
100ml (4fl oz) milk
Salt and pepper to taste

Place chops in bottom of baking dish. Layer potatoes and onions on top of chops. Mix mushroom soup with Parmesan cheese, milk and spices. Pour over chops. Cover with clingfilm and cook at 70% power for 20–25 minutes. Rearrange midway through cooking time.

Leg of Lamb with Potatoes
Serve with mint jelly

2.25–3.25kg (5–7lb) leg of lamb
(excess fat removed)
3–4 garlic cloves
1 × 15ml tbsp (1tbsp) vegetable oil
1 × 15ml tbsp (1tbsp) bottled
browning sauce

1 × 2.5ml tsp (½tsp) freshly
ground pepper
450g (1lb) new potatoes

Make slits over entire surface of lamb every 7.5cm (3in) and insert small pieces of garlic in slits. Rub lamb with combined vegetable oil and browning sauce. Sprinkle with pepper. Place lamb with thick side down on roasting rack. Cover loosely with greaseproof paper. Cook at 50% power for 11 minutes per 450g (1lb) for medium. Turn meat over halfway through cooking (unless your oven requires more turning.) While roast is standing, place potatoes in fat from roast and cook on HIGH for 5–8 minutes.

If using temperature probe, insert in thickest portion of meat without touching bone. Cook to 75°C (170°F) for medium to well-done lamb.

Ten-minute Beef Stroganoff

Serves 4 to 5

450g (1lb) round or rump steak
1 × 75g (3oz) can mushroom slices
with liquid
1 packet dry onion soup mix
225ml (8fl oz) sour cream

2 × 15ml tbsp (2tbsp) ketchup
Pinch of garlic powder
40g (1½oz) butter
2 × 15ml tbsp (2tbsp) flour

Trim fat from meat. Cut meat diagonally across the grain in very thin strips. (It is easier to cut thinly if meat is slightly frozen first.) Melt butter for 45–60 seconds on HIGH. Add meat and cook for 3 minutes on HIGH. Add 150ml (6fl oz) water and mushrooms. Stir in soup mix and heat to boiling. Mix sour cream with flour, stirring to blend. Add hot mixture. Add ketchup and garlic powder. Cook on 70% power until mixture thickens. Do not overcook or meat will be tough. Serve over rice or noodles.

Pizza Crust

Makes two 30cm (12in) crusts

225ml (8fl oz) warm water
1 sachet active dry yeast
25g (1oz) lard or margarine

1 × 2.5ml tsp (½tsp) salt
450g (1lb) strong plain flour
1 × 15ml tbsp (1tbsp) salad oil

Place warm water and yeast in mixing bowl or food processor. Add shortening, salt and half the flour. Mix well until smooth. Gradually add remaining flour until stiff dough is formed. Knead by hand 8–10 minutes, or process for 30 seconds, using sharp blade of your food processor. Check, and if dough is not smooth and elastic, continue to process in 15 second bursts until the desired consistency is reached. Place in greased bowl and cover with clingfilm. Speed up rising if desired by microwaving for 6 minutes on 10% power and allowing to stand 10 minutes before repeating process. When double in size (60 minutes if not speeding up rising), punch down and divide in half. Roll out and place on greased 30cm (12in) pizza pan. Add pizza sauce, along with your favourite fillings, such as Mozzarella cheese, anchovies, sausage, green pepper, onion, mushrooms, etc. Cook conventionally for 20–25 minutes in preheated 225°C (450°F) oven.

Pizza Filling

Serves 4
Makes enough for two 30cm (12in) pizzas

1 × 15ml tbsp (1tbsp) salad oil
1 medium chopped onion
4 garlic cloves, minced
1 × 525g (1lb 3oz) can tomatoes
1 × 225g (8oz) bottle tomato sauce

1 bay leaf
1 × 5ml tsp (1tsp) each salt, oregano and basil
1 × 15ml tbsp (1tbsp) sugar
Pepper to taste
Meat and other toppings to taste

Microwave onion and garlic cloves in oil for 2–3 minutes on HIGH. Add remaining ingredients and microwave 15 minutes on HIGH. Reduce to 50% power for 10 minutes. (Simmering helps develop good flavour.)

Beef Burgundy

Serves 6

675g (1½lb) sirloin
Freshly ground black pepper
3 garlic cloves, crushed
25g (1oz) bacon fat or oil
1 medium onion, thinly sliced
225g (½lb) fresh mushrooms, sliced
225ml (8fl oz) sour cream

2 × 15ml tbsp (2tbsp) flour
75g (3oz) mature Cheddar cheese, grated
100ml (4fl oz) Burgundy or red wine of choice
Pinch of basil, marjoram and thyme
2 × 5ml tsp (2tsp) salt

Cut steak in very thin slices across the grain. (It is easier to cut if meat is partially frozen.) Combine garlic cloves, onion, mushrooms, wine and seasonings and cook in a covered dish for 5 minutes on HIGH. Blend flour with sour cream and add to seasoning mixture and allow to cook for 5–8 additional minutes on 70% power. Set aside and cook steak in bacon fat or oil on HIGH 3–4 minutes. Stir halfway through cooking. Add sauce mixture and cheese to beef and stir to blend. Cook 1–3 minutes longer on 70% power. Serve over noodles or rice. Garnish with sautéd mushroom slices and chopped fresh parsley.

Sausage and Rice Casserole

Serves 5 to 6

150g (6oz) raw weight long-grain rice, cooked
450g (1lb) sausage meat
1 large onion, peeled and chopped
250ml (½pt) chicken stock

225g (½lb) fresh mushrooms or 2 × 84g (3oz) cans
50ml (2fl oz) single cream
2 × 15ml tbsp (2tbsp) flour

Place crumbled sausage into a casserole. Microwave on HIGH 5–6 minutes until done. (Do not overcook.) Drain on paper towel and remove all but 2 × 15ml tbsp (2tbsp) of fat from casserole. Sauté onions and mushrooms for 3–4 minutes on HIGH. Add flour and stir to blend. Add cream and chicken stock. Cook for 4–5 minutes until thickened. Add seasonings and combine all ingredients. Pour into casserole and microwave on 70% power for 10–15 minutes.

Mongolian Beef

Serves 4

450g (1lb) sliced sirloin steak
1 large onion, grated
8–10 cloves garlic, finely crushed

2 × 15ml tbsp (2tbsp) oil
2 × 5ml tsp (2tsp) sesame oil
1 × 2.5ml tsp (½tsp) salt

Marinade:
4 × 15ml tbsp (4tbsp) soy sauce
1 × 15ml tbsp (1tbsp) dry sherry
1 × 5ml tsp (1tsp) black pepper
3 × 15ml tbsp (3tbsp) cold water

2 × 15ml tbsp (2tbsp) cornflour
1 × 5ml tsp (1tsp) sugar
1 × 15ml tbsp (1tbsp) oil

Slice the steak in very thin slices across the grain. (It is easier to slice if meat is partially frozen.) Combine marinade ingredients in a bowl, add sliced beef, mix thoroughly and set aside for at least 30 minutes. Meat-marinade combination may be refrigerated overnight or frozen for later use. Microwave the oil, garlic and beef, covered, about 3 minutes on HIGH. Stir in 2 × 15ml tbsp (2tbsp) soy sauce. Microwave onion, covered, 1 minute and stir in meat. Microwave 1 minute longer, add 2 × 5ml tsp (1tsp) sesame oil. Serve with noodles.

Marinated Barbecued Pork Chops

Serves 4

100ml (4fl oz) vegetable oil
50ml (2fl oz) olive oil
50ml (2fl oz) lemon juice
3 cloves garlic, crushed
1 × 5ml tsp (1tsp) salt

1 × 5ml tsp (1tsp) paprika
1 × 2.5ml tsp (½tsp) pepper
6 bay leaves
Four 2.5cm (1in) thick loin or rib
    pork chops

Combine all ingredients except meat in a shallow baking dish and mix well. Add meat to marinade; cover and marinate overnight in refrigerator. Preheat browning grill 8 or 9 minutes (or as manufacturer directs) and cook 5 minutes on first side and 5–6 minutes on second side.

Liver and Onions

Serves 4 to 5

4–6 slices bacon cut in thirds
25g (1oz) flour
1 × 5ml tsp (1tsp) salt
1 × 5ml tsp (1tsp) black pepper

450g (1lb) liver (sliced into
  serving-sized pieces)
2 large onions, thinly sliced
100ml (4fl oz) water

Microwave bacon in a 30cm × 20cm (12 × 8in) dish on HIGH for 4–6 minutes. While bacon cooks, combine flour with salt and pepper. Dredge liver in flour, sprinkling excess flour over pieces. Set aside. Remove all but 2 × 15ml tbsp (2tbsp) bacon fat and place liver in dish. Add onions and water, saving bacon to be crumbled over liver at end of cooking time. Cover with clingfilm and microwave on HIGH 5 minutes. Reduce power to 50% and microwave 10–15 minutes until fork tender. Turn liver over and rearrange after first half of cooking time.

Meat Loaf

Serves 5 to 6

675g (1½lb) lean minced beef
2 eggs, well beaten
1 medium onion, chopped
2 sticks celery, thinly sliced
2 × 15ml tbsp (2tbsp) green
  pepper, chopped
2 carrots, finely grated

1 × 15ml tbsp (1tbsp) horseradish
1 × 5ml tsp (1tsp) dry mustard
1 × 15ml tbsp (1tbsp) parsley
1 × 5ml tsp (1tsp) garlic salt
1 × 2.5ml tsp (½tsp) pepper
3 × 15ml tbsp (3tbsp) ketchup

Toss all ingredients (except ketchup) gently with two forks. Place meat mixture in a 25cm (10in) round baking dish with an inverted cup or glass in centre. (A ring mould may also be used.) Cook for 5 minutes on HIGH and 10–15 minutes on 50% power. During last several minutes add ketchup. Allow to stand 5 minutes before serving.

☞ If you would like to serve the meat loaf ring on another plate after 5 minutes standing time cover with plate and invert the ring. Add additional ketchup and garnish with herbs and parsley.

Taglarina
A good dish to prepare ahead and freeze

Serves 12 to 15

900g (2lb) lean minced beef
1 medium-sized onion, chopped
4 cloves garlic, crushed
1 pepper, chopped
1 × 15ml tbsp (1tbsp) chilli powder
1 × 5ml tbsp (1tsp) basil
1 × 2.5ml tsp (½tsp) oregano
1 × 15ml tbsp (1tbsp) Worcestershire sauce
1 × 15ml tbsp (1tbsp) sugar
1 × 5ml tsp (1tsp) salt
1 × 2.5ml tsp (½tsp) pepper
1 × 400g (16oz) can tomatoes
1 × 400g (16oz) can sweetcorn, drained
1 × 225g (8oz) bottle tomato sauce
1 × 100g (4oz) can ripe olives, sliced and olive juice
150–225g (6–8oz) spaghetti, cooked
150g (6oz) Cheddar cheese, grated

Place minced beef, onion, garlic and pepper in a 2 litre (3½pt) glass measure and cook for 10–12 minutes on HIGH. Drain and add seasonings, tomatoes, corn and tomato sauce. Add olives and olive juice. Taste and adjust seasonings. Add spaghetti, stirring to blend. Pour into 2 casserole dishes. (This is better if flavours are allowed to blend overnight in the refrigerator.) Cook each dish for 10–12 minutes at 70% power or until hot.

Quick Barbecue Burgers

Serves 8

450g (1lb) minced beef
1 medium-sized onion, chopped
1 stick celery, finely chopped
2 × 15ml tbsp (2tbsp) green pepper
1 × 2.5ml tsp (½tsp) garlic salt
Pepper
100–150ml (4–6fl oz) barbecue sauce
8 hamburger buns, toasted

Place minced beef, onion, celery and green pepper in a casserole and microwave on HIGH for 5–8 minutes, stirring occasionally. Add remaining ingredients and cook on 50% power covered for 4–5 minutes. Spoon over buns and serve immediately.

🐑 Use the microwave as a big time saver by combination cooking. Microwave meats first in the microwave, finishing up on the grill or barbecue.

Ribs of Beef
Could be a Father's Day speciality

Serves 4 to 6
2kg (4lb) joint ribs of beef

Place beef fat side down on a rack or inverted saucer placed in a baking dish. (Shield tail of roast if roast weighs over 2.25kg (5lb).) Make sure roast always stays out of juices, because this will produce a steamed or pot-roast flavour. Estimate total cooking time following chart below:

	Min 450g/lb	Removal Temperature
Rare	9–12	55°C (130°F)
Medium	10–14	65°C (150°F)
Well done	11–15	72°C (165°F)

Work out total cooking time and divide in half. Microwave on HIGH for 7–8 minutes. Microwave remainder of first half at 50% power. Turn roast with fat side up and insert microwave thermometer if desired. Cook at 50% power until temperature reaches desired level. Remove from oven, cover with foil and allow to stand 10–20 minutes before serving.

Stuffed Green Peppers

Serves 4

4 large green peppers
450g (1lb) lean minced beef
1 medium onion, peeled and chopped
1 stick celery, chopped
1 × 400g (16oz) bottle tomato sauce

250g (9oz) long-grained rice, cooked
2 garlic cloves, crushed
1 × 5ml tsp (1tsp) salt
1 × 2.5ml tsp (½tsp) basil
Freshly ground black pepper

Prepare peppers by cutting a thin slice from the stem end. Remove seeds with a teaspoon. Combine beef and onions in a glass casserole and cook for 3–5 minutes on HIGH. Combine minced beef and onions with remaining ingredients, mixing well. Stuff peppers with mixture and place on baking dish, covering tightly with clingfilm. Microwave 12–16 minutes on 70% power.

Onion Mushroom Sauce
Delicious served with grilled steak

450g (1lb) fresh mushrooms, sliced
1 large onion, peeled and thinly
  sliced
50g (2oz) butter
100ml (4fl oz) white wine
3 × 15ml tbsp (3tbsp)
  Worcestershire sauce

3 × 15ml tbsp (3tbsp) soy sauce
1 × 2.5ml tsp (½tsp) oregano
Pinch of garlic salt
Pinch of rosemary
1 × 15ml tbsp (1tbsp) fresh parsley

Microwave mushrooms for 2–3 minutes on HIGH. Drain and add remaining ingredients cooking for 5–6 minutes on 30% power. Spoon over steak or serve as a side dish.

Italian-style Sloppy Joes

Serves 6

450g (1lb) minced beef
1 medium-sized onion, peeled and
  chopped
1 × 225g (8oz) bottle tomato
  sauce
25g (1oz) Parmesan cheese
40g (1½oz) grated mature
  Cheddar cheese

Pinch of oregano
Pinch of basil
Pinch of garlic powder
Salt and pepper to taste
6 hamburger buns
6 slices Mozzarella cheese

Crumble minced beef in a casserole and microwave on HIGH 5–7 minutes. Stir occasionally to break up meat; drain. Add remaining ingredients, except buns and Mozzarella cheese. Cook on HIGH 2–3 minutes until mixture starts to simmer. Microwave on 50% power for 4–6 minutes, stirring once. Spoon mixture on bottom half of bun and top with slice of Mozzarella cheese and bun top. Serve at once.

🕅 Boneless meats cook more evenly than meats with a bone because the bone attracts microwave energy.

🕅 To remove stains and brown spots from browning dish, use bicarbonate of soda.

Marinated Steak

Marinate steak first for 4–6 hours and then cook on the browning grill

Serves 3 to 4

675g (1½lb) sirloin steak
325ml (12fl oz) salad oil
50ml (2fl oz) Worcestershire sauce
Salt
100ml (4fl oz) vinegar
2 × 5ml tsp (2tsp) garlic salt

150ml (6fl oz) soy sauce
2 × 15ml tbsp (2tbsp) mustard
1 × 15ml tbsp (1tbsp) black pepper
1 × 5ml tsp (1tsp) dried parsley
65ml (2½fl oz) lemon juice

Place all of above ingredients, except steak, into a blender. Blend until contents are thoroughly mixed (about 30 seconds). Mix in a shaker if a blender is not available. Place steak in a glass container and pour marinade over it. Cover container and place in the refrigerator for 4–6 hours. This marinade may be refrigerated and used over again.

Preheat browning grill or skillet for 8–9 minutes on HIGH or according to manufacturer's instructions. While grill is preheating drain steak and blot with paper towel. Add 2 pats of butter to preheated grill and microwave for 3 minutes on first side and 2–3 minutes on second side for a medium-rare steak.

🍳 This marinade may be stored in the refrigerator for up to 2 months. However, after beef roast or steak has been marinated in it, do not refrigerate and use for longer than 3 weeks.

🍳 Marinate lean tender cuts of meat for several hours, or overnight. Add slightly less liquid than if cooking conventionally and cover tightly with clingfilm. Slower cooking tenderises meat. Use a setting of 50% power or below.

Simply Scrumptious
Clay Pot Cookery

General Guidelines

The use of the clay pot in the microwave is a combination of two excellent cooking methods. The clay pot is one of the oldest cooking utensils and the microwave is one of the fastest methods of cooking.

The clay pot is porous and should be soaked before each use. The clay pot then slowly releases the water during the cooking process. Less tender cuts of meat become tender, dried beans become a gourmet delight, and speciality dishes become simple and delicious.

The clay pot instruction book should be followed concerning soaking times. The first time the clay pot is used the soaking time is longer.

Be sure the clay pot you are using is suitable for use in the microwave. Try the one-minute test by placing an empty clay pot in the microwave for one minute on HIGH. If the clay pot is hot to the touch at the end of the minute time period, the pot is not designed for use in the microwave. Many manufacturers recom-

111

mend placing a cup of water in the oven when testing the micro-wave safety of a dish. Some microwave ovens can be operated for a short period of time empty. Check the instruction manual.

A general rule of thumb for cooking meat items is 5 minutes per 450g (lb) on HIGH and 15 minutes per 450g (lb) on 50% power. Food should stand covered at least 5 minutes before serving.

The basic principles of microwave cookery should also be followed when cooking with a clay pot.

Mezetti

An all-time favourite! Try it and be prepared to have many more requests for this dish

Serves 6 to 8

450g (1lb) minced beef	2.5ml tsp (½tsp) paprika
1 medium onion, finely chopped	1 × 5ml tsp (1tsp) salt
2 × 15ml tbsp (2tbsp) green pepper, chopped	1 × 283g (10oz) can tomato soup
1 stick celery, chopped	1 × 283g (10oz) can mushroom soup
225g (8oz) fine egg noodles	1 × 100g (4oz) can mushrooms, drained
2 garlic cloves, crushed	200ml (8fl oz) water
1–3 × 5ml tsp (1–3tsp) chilli powder (season to taste)	75g (3oz) cheddar cheese, shredded

Place minced beef, green pepper, onion, celery and garlic in water-soaked clay pot. Cover with water-soaked lid. Cook on HIGH for 6 minutes. Drain off excess liquid. Sprinkle noodles on meat mixture. Stir together chilli powder, paprika, salt, tomato soup, mushroom soup, mushrooms and water in a bowl. Pour mixture over meat and noodles. Re-cover and microwave on HIGH for 10 minutes and on 50% power for 15 to 18 minutes or until noodles are cooked. Sprinkle cheese on top and cover. Let stand 5 minutes.

Chicken or Turkey Stock

900g (2lb) chicken necks, backs,
  and wings (or turkey parts)
3 sticks celery
3 carrots, washed but not scraped

1 medium onion
6 peppercorns (or 1 × 5ml tsp
  (1tsp) black pepper)
1 × 7.5ml tsp (1½tsp) salt

Combine all ingredients in water-soaked clay pot. Fill with water within 5cm (2in) of top. Cover and microwave in water-soaked clay pot for 15 minutes on HIGH and then reduce to 50% power for 45 minutes, or until done.

Stuffed Chicken with Rice

1–1.5kg (2–3lb) fryer
150g (6oz) Quick-cooking long-
  grain rice

300ml (12fl oz) water
1 medium onion, chopped
1 stick celery, chopped

Stuff chicken cavity with onion and celery. Place chicken in water-soaked clay pot breast side down. Cover with water-soaked lid. Microwave on HIGH for 10 minutes. Remove chicken. Add rice and water to cooker and stir to blend. Place chicken breast side up and cook 30 to 45 minutes on 70% power, or until chicken is tender. Let stand covered 5 minutes.

Southern-style Green Beans

400ml (16fl oz) water
3 slices bacon, cut in small pieces
1 medium onion, chopped
1 × 5ml tsp (1tsp) beef stock

1 × 15ml tbsp (1tbsp) bacon fat
1 × 5ml tsp (1tsp) salt
675–900g (1½–2lb) green beans,
  cut in half and trimmed

Combine water, bacon, onion and stock in water-soaked clay pot. Microwave on HIGH 5 to 7 minutes until water is very hot. Add beans, salt and bacon fat to hot water. Cover with water-soaked lid. Microwave on HIGH 5 minutes. Stir and re-cover. Cook on 50% power 40 to 50 minutes. Let stand, covered, 5 minutes.

Beans à la Delicious
A plain bean is turned into a gourmet delight

450g (1lb) Pinto dried beans
1.1 litre (2pt) water
1 large onion, chopped
1 garlic clove, crushed
1 × 5ml tsp (1tsp) salt
Pinch of white pepper
1 ham bone

Rinse beans and place in a deep dish. Cover with 5cm (2in) of water. Microwave on HIGH until water comes to the boil and boil rapidly for 2 mintues. Let stand for 1 hour or more. Drain water into measuring jug and add enough to make 1.1 litre (2pt).

Place all ingredients in water-soaked clay pot. Stir well. Cover with water-soaked clay lid. Microwave 15 minutes on HIGH. Stir and cover. Microwave for 30 to 35 minutes on 50% power. Stir and cover. Continue to cook on 50% power for 60 to 65 minutes or until beans are tender. Let stand 10 minutes.

Barbecued Pork Ribs
Quick, easy, and delicious

1.5kg (3lb) pork ribs (small meaty
ribs should be used)

Sauce:
100ml (4fl oz) barbecue sauce
50ml (2fl oz) tomato sauce
1 × 5ml tsp (1tsp) dried parsley
flakes
1 medium onion, finely chopped

Place ribs in water-soaked clay pot. Cook for 15 minutes on HIGH. Drain off all liquid. Cover ribs in sauce. Cook for 25 minutes on 50% power. Turn ribs and baste with sauce. Cook 20 minutes more on 50% power.

🐷 If ribs are prepared ahead of time, slice into individual ribs and place in glass casserole dish. Baste ribs with sauce. Reheat for 5 to 10 minutes on 80% power, serve, eat, and enjoy!

Poussin with Rice

150g (6oz) Uncle Ben's long-grain rice
100ml (4fl oz) water
225g (½lb) mushrooms (sliced)
1 × 295g (10oz) can condensed mushroom soup

2 poussins (weight to total 900g–1.1kg (2 to 2½lb))
Salt to taste

Combine all ingredients except poussins in water-soaked clay pot. Stir thoroughly. Place poussins on top of mixture. Add salt to taste. Cover with water-soaked lid and microwave 15 minutes on HIGH. Turn poussins over and stir rice mixture – especially around the outside edges of clay pot. Microwave for 30 to 35 minutes on 50% power, or until rice and poussins are done. Let stand 5 minutes.

Pork Chops with Sauerkraut

Serves 4 to 6

4 to 6 pork chops (approximately 1kg/2lb)
2 onions sliced in rings
1 × 764g (27oz) can sauerkraut, well drained and rinsed
2 large potatoes, sliced
2 large apples, sliced
100ml (4fl oz) white wine

2 × 5ml tsp (2tsp) chicken stock
1 × 5ml tsp (1tsp) caraway seeds (optional)
1 × 15ml tbsp (1tbsp) parsley flakes
1 × 2.5ml tsp (½tsp) black pepper
100g (4oz) salt pork, finely diced

Place all ingredients except chops in water-soaked clay pot. Stir well. Place pork chops on top of mixture. Cover with water-soaked lid. Cook for 15 minutes on HIGH. Turn pork chops and stir mixture gently. Cook 45 to 55 minutes on 50% power or until pork chops are tender. Let stand 5 minutes before serving.

♉ If arcing occurs in your oven, turn oven off immediately; this can cause damage to the oven interior surface or cooking utensil. Arcing is an electrical current which flows from the wall of the oven to a metal object in the oven, causing a light flash and popping sound. Improper metal usage causes the problem.

115

Porcupines
Children, especially, love this

Serves 4 to 6

900g (1lb) minced beef
1 medium onion, chopped
1 × 1.25ml tsp (¼tsp) celery seeds
1 × 2.5ml tsp (½tsp) salt
1 × 2.5ml tsp (½tsp) garlic salt
Pepper
50g (2oz) uncooked rice

2 × 15ml tbsp (2tbsp) green
  pepper, chopped
1 × 5ml tsp (1tsp) Worcestershire
  sauce
1 × 283g (10oz) can tomato soup
50ml (2fl oz) water

Mix all ingredients except tomato soup and water in mixing bowl. Shape into meatballs (about 3.75cm (1½in) diameter). Put meatballs in water-soaked pot and cover with water-soaked lid. Microwave on HIGH for 5 minutes. Drain liquid. Mix tomato soup and water and pour over meatballs. Re-cover and microwave for 30 to 35 minutes on 50% power, or until meatballs are done. Let stand 5 minutes.

Chilli

Serves 6 to 8

450g (1lb) minced beef
1 large onion, chopped
½ green pepper, chopped
4 sticks celery, chopped (optional)
2 garlic cloves, crushed
1 × 452g (16oz) can tomatoes,
  mashed
1 × 226g (8oz) bottle tomato
  sauce

1–3 × 15ml tsp (1–3tsp) chilli
  powder
1 × 340g (12oz) can V-8 juice
225ml (8fl oz) water
1 × 5ml tsp (1tsp) basil
1 × 5ml tsp (1tsp) salt
1 × 15ml tbsp (1tbsp) paprika
2 × 450g (1lb) cans beans drained
  (chilli or kidney)

Place minced beef, onion, pepper, celery and garlic in water-soaked clay pot. Cover and microwave on HIGH for 7 to 10 minutes. Drain off excess liquid. Add remaining ingredients, except beans. Re-cover and cook 30 minutes on 50% power. Add beans and stir well. Continue to cook 10 minutes on 50% power. Let stand, covered, 5 minutes.

Simply Scrumptious
Breads

General Guidelines

You will find that the microwave can be an asset when baking bread, saving time and energy. You may use it most effectively by combining microwave and conventional cooking. Some of the recipes in this section are designed especially for complimentary cooking, taking the best from both worlds.

Listed below are tips to aid in successful bread making:

If your oven has an uneven cooking pattern, when proving or baking bread, place the bread dish on an inverted saucer to give more even cooking results.

If your microwave has a probe, use it when heating milk or water so the yeast will work most effectively.

For most microwave baking use medium power or a 50% setting.

Grease dishes lightly and sprinkle with crumbs. The crumbs absorb excess moisture which forms between the bread and the dish during microwaving.

Do not overcook. Overcooked breads are tough.

To speed rising, use the following as a guide:

10% power	—	Microwave 10 to 12 minutes and allow to rest 15 minutes. Repeat if necessary. (Use this power level if your microwave has an uneven cooking pattern.)
30% power	—	Microwave 1 to 2 minutes and allow to stand 15 minutes.
50% power	—	Microwave 1 minute and let stand for 15 minutes. Repeat if necessary.

Croûtons

4 slices bread from a thick-sliced
  loaf, cubed

1 × 15ml tbsp (1tbsp) garlic herb
  seasoning

Place bread cubes in a round dish such as a pie dish. Sprinkle with seasoning. Cook on HIGH for 6–8 minutes, stirring every two minutes.

Quick Butter Biscuits

This is a great recipe to use conventionally also.
These biscuits are very good warmed in the microwave

Makes twelve 50cm (2in) biscuits
100g (4oz) butter (firm)
225g (8oz) self-raising flour

150ml (¼pt) cold milk

Cut butter into flour and add milk. Knead several times. Roll out and cut into biscuits. Preheat browning tray 6 minutes. Place biscuits in circle and cook for 1 minute on HIGH. Turn over and cook 1–1½ minutes on HIGH.

Magic Buttermilk Muffins
Tasty as a quick breakfast bread

Makes 3 dozen
100g (4oz) 100% bran
225ml (8fl oz) boiling water
100g (4oz) butter
100ml (4fl oz) oil
325g (12oz) sugar
2 eggs
275g (10oz) sifted all-purpose
  flour
2 × 5ml tsp (2tsp) bicarbonate of
  soda
1 × 5ml tsp (1tsp) salt
225g (8oz) All-Bran cereal
400ml (16fl oz) buttermilk
150g (6oz) raisins or chopped
  dates

Boil water in glass cup in microwave. Pour over 100% bran and allow to cool. Set aside. Cream butter, oil and sugar. Add eggs, one at a time, beating well after each addition. Add flour, bicarbonate of soda, salt and buttermilk, mixing well. Add bran, raisins and nuts. Stir only until well mixed. Place cup-cake cases in custard cups or in microwave-safe muffin pan. Fill half-full with batter and cook 2½–3 minutes on HIGH. Cover with clingfilm when removing from oven and allow to stand several minutes. This mixture will keep in a covered container up to 5 or 6 weeks in the refrigerator. Just use as needed; do not stir.

Herb Bread Sticks

100g (4oz) butter, softened
1 × 2.5ml tsp (½tsp) each of
  chives, tarragon, marjoram,
  parsley, garlic salt

2 × 15ml tbsp (2tbsp) sesame
  seeds
¾ loaf very thin bread

Soften butter for 30 seconds on 50% power. Add spices and sesame seeds. Spread on bread. Cut each piece of bread into 4 fingers and microwave for 5–8 minutes stirring every 2 minutes. Enjoy with salads and soups.

Potato Rolls

These rolls could be called 'never fail' and work very nicely using combination microwave and conventional cookery. Good to microwave to brown-and-serve stage, then freeze and cook conventionally later – and still have that fresh yeast bread taste!

Makes 2½ to 3 dozen
225ml (8fl oz) milk
2 × 15ml tbsp (2tbsp) honey
1 × 15ml tbsp (1tbsp) salt
65g (2½oz) butter, melted
225ml (8fl oz) warm water
  (105°F–115°F.)
1 sachet active dry yeast
2 eggs
1 medium potato (or 1 cup mashed
  potatoes)
100g (4oz) Miller's bran (or raw
  unprocessed wholewheat flour)

500–625g (1lb 2oz–1lb 6oz) plain flour

Bake potato: Microwave pricked, well-scrubbed potato 4–5 minutes on HIGH and wrap in foil to stand several minutes. Peel and mash.

Prepare dough: Dissolve yeast in warm water. Combine milk, honey, salt, butter and well beaten eggs. Add mashed potato. Then add yeast-water mixture, Miller's bran and 225g (8oz) of flour. Beat well for several minutes. Stir in enough flour to produce a slightly stiff dough. Turn dough out onto a lightly floured pastry cloth or board and knead until smooth and elastic, 8–10 minutes. Add only enough flour to keep dough from sticking to board or cloth. (On rainy days more flour will be required to keep from sticking.) Place dough in bowl that has been oiled with 2–3 × 15ml tbsp (2–3tbsp) of cooking oil. Turn dough over once so that all sides are greased. Cover with clingfilm and allow to rise until double in bulk, about 1 hour.

If you would like to speed up the rising process, place bread in glass or microwave-safe bowl in microwave and warm for 10–12 minutes on 10% power. Let stand for 10 minutes and repeat process if desired.

Microwave Cookery

Punch dough down and turn out onto worktop and form a smooth ball. Pinch dough into 36 small balls, placing onto three well greased 23cm (9in) pie plates. Cover tightly with clingfilm and allow to rise until double in bulk. (Use speeded up rise process if desired). Cook each for 5–6 minutes on 50% power until set. At this point cool and freeze, to be enjoyed later by heating or browning conventionally.

Conventionally

Punch dough down and make out into rolls. Cover and let rise until double in bulk – about 45 minutes. Bake at 200°C (400°F, Gas mark 6) for 15–20 minutes. This recipe works well as a refrigerator-type roll. Make dough and place in refrigerator. Make out into rolls the next day, following the same procedure for rising process.

How to Defrost Frozen Bread Dough

Microwave 325ml (12fl oz) of water until boiling in a baking dish such as 30cm × 20cm (12 × 8in.)

Heavily grease a 20cm × 10cm × 12.5cm (8 × 4 × 5in) loaf dish. Cut a piece of greaseproof paper to fit and place in loaf dish. Grease the top of the paper. Butter frozen dough on all sides and place in loaf dish.

Put loaf dish in the 30cm × 20cm (12 × 8in) baking dish with the hot water.

Cover with greaseproof paper and microwave for 2 minutes on 50% power. Turn dough over and microwave for 2 additional minutes.

Allow to stand 2 minutes. Dough should be defrosted and slightly warm. If not, microwave 1 minute at a time, turning dough over each time until thawed.

🖐 When warming any type of bread, place first on a paper towel or cloth napkin so moisture trapped between bread and oven floor will be absorbed. Remember bread will toughen if over-heated. One roll may be warmed in only 8–12 seconds.

Bonanza Bread
Nutritious and delicious.
Goes well with cream cheese

Makes 2 loaves

100g (4oz) sifted plain flour
100g (4oz) wholewheat flour
1 × 2.5ml tsp (½tsp) salt
1 × 2.5ml tsp (½tsp) bicarbonate
of soda
1 × 3.75ml tsp (1½tsp) baking
powder
75g (3oz) dried skimmed milk
25g (1oz) wheatgerm
75g (3oz) firmly packed brown
sugar

75g (3oz) mixed nuts (pecans,
peanuts, walnuts, etc)
75g (3oz) raisins or dates
3 eggs
100ml (4fl oz) vegetable oil
100ml (4fl oz) treacle
150ml (¼pt) orange juice
2 medium-sized bananas, mashed
50g (2oz) chopped dried apricots

Mix flours, salt, bicarbonate of soda, baking powder, dried milk, wheatgerm, sugar, nuts and raisins thoroughly with fork. Use food processor or blender to mix eggs, oil, treacle, orange juice and bananas; add apricots and process to chop coarsely. Combine two mixtures together and stir just until all flour is moistened and blended. Prepare two standard loaf dishes, by greasing well and place greaseproof paper on bottom of dish. Cook each loaf separately for 9 minutes at 50% power and for 3–5 minutes on HIGH. Cover with clingfilm when removing from oven so moisture won't be lost. When cool, wrap tightly and store overnight, allowing flavours to mellow.

For proving or baking, placing the bread dish on an inverted saucer may give more even cooking results.

Simply Scrumptious
Cakes

General Guidelines

Microwave-baked cakes are lighter and moister than conventional cakes. They microwave in one-sixth to one-third of the time needed conventionally.

Dish Preparation: No preparation is needed if the cake is to be served from the dish. If the cake is to be removed from the dish, line the bottom of the dish with 2 layers of greaseproof paper for easy removal. When baking a bundt cake, plain or fluted, grease the dish well with oil, butter or margarine and coat with granulated sugar, crushed digestive biscuits or dry toasted breadcrumbs. Never use flour for coating; it will become sticky and lumpy during cooking.

    Baking Dish: Always think 'round' for more even cooking results. Round dishes allow more even cooking than square ones. When square dishes are required, as when baking brownies or other cake squares, place a triangle of aluminium foil over each corner to 'shield' it from overcooking. Rectangular dishes are not recommended for most even cooking results. Bundt and ring dishes give good results. If you do not have a glass or plastic tube

123

cake dish, you can create one by inverting glass or jar in a round casserole or heat-tempered glass bowl.

Baking: Fill the dish no more than half-full. Use excess batter for cupcakes. Because of the short baking time, microwaved cakes will not brown. By using frostings, icings, glazes, sauces and toppings, cakes may look appealing and quite often no different than conventionally baked. Bake cake layers separately, one at a time. Cakes are often microwaved at a reduced power level: 50%–70% to rise, and finished on HIGH to set the batter.

Testing that Cake is Cooked: As in conventional baking, cakes are done when a knife inserted near the centre comes out clean, or when the top springs back when lightly pressed with a finger. The cake will usually start coming away from the edge of the dish. Unlike conventional cakes, the microwave cake should always appear slightly moist on top after baking. There should be a damp spot in the centre. This moisture will disappear when the cake stands 2 or 3 minutes. If it does not, touch the damp spot with your finger. Sometimes the dampness you see is only moisture on the surface that has not evaporated. If so, it will usually stick to your finger and you can see the 'done' cake beneath. If you continue cooking until the damp spot disappears, the cake will be overcooked and tough.

Standing Time: Consider standing time part of the cooking process. After taking the cake from the cooker, let it stand directly on the oven top 5–10 minutes. This helps the cake complete baking on the bottom. Never use a cooling rack. If you are uncertain it is cooked when you test the cake, take it out of the oven and test again after standing time. The cake may be put back in the oven and baked more after standing time, if needed. Cover the cake with greaseproof paper or clingfilm during standing time and after the cake is inverted, until it cools, to retain moisture in the cake. (You may want to leave the cake dish inverted on top of the cake while it is cooling.)

Converting Conventional Recipes to Microwaving: Plain cakes, chocolate or spice cakes convert well. Sponge cakes cannot be microwave-baked successfully because they require dry heat. They will rise, but will not develop the crust needed to hold their shape when removed from the oven.

Sour Cream Pound Cake

225g (8oz) butter
675g (1½lb) sugar
325g (12oz) flour
1 × 1.25ml tsp (¼tsp) bicarbonate
   of soda
1 × 2.5ml tsp (½tsp) baking
   powder
225ml (8fl oz) sour cream
6 eggs
2 × 5ml tsp (2tsp) flavouring
   (vanilla, lemon or almond, etc.)

Cream butter and sugar. Add eggs and beat until light and fluffy. Sift dry ingredients together and add to sugar mixture alternately with sour cream. Add flavouring. Pour into prepared 2.5 litre (4½pt) bundt dish (greased generously and coated with digestive biscuit crumbs). Microwave on 70% power for 15–18 minutes or until done. Cover with greaseproof paper and let stand 10–15 minutes on oven top. Invert.

Variations: Sour Cream Pound Cake is a good basic recipe. Delicious variations of pound cake may be made by following this basic recipe and making the following additions and substitutions.

Coconut Pound Cake: Fold in 150g (6oz) grated fresh coconut and flavour the cake with 1 × 5ml tsp (1tsp) almond essence.
Chocolate Pound Cake: Add 25g (1oz) cocoa to dry ingredients.
Brown Sugar Pound Cake: Instead of 675g (1½lb) sugar use 450g (1lb) light brown sugar and 225g (8oz) white sugar. Also add 75g (3oz) finely chopped walnuts. After baked and inverted from dish, top with walnut glaze. To make glaze, cream 100g (4oz) sifted icing sugar and 25g (1oz) butter. Add 6 × 15ml tbsp (6tbsp) cream, few drops vanilla essence and 40g (1½oz) chopped walnuts. Blend well. After baking cake, invert from dish and top with Walnut Glaze.
Strawberry Pound Cake. Substitute 225g (8oz) puréed fresh strawberries for sour cream. If using frozen, sweetened strawberries, reduce sugar to 600g (1lb 6oz).

Date Nut Party Cake

Makes one 20cm (8in) layer

75g (3oz) dates
100ml (4fl oz) boiling water
1 × 2.5ml tsp (½tsp) bicarbonate
  of soda
100ml (4fl oz) mayonnaise
100g (4oz) sugar

1 egg
100g (4oz) flour
1 × 1.25ml tsp (¼tsp) cinnamon
50g (2oz) walnuts, finely chopped
1 × 15ml tbsp (1tbsp) cocoa

Combine dates, water and bicarbonate of soda and set aside. Beat mayonnaise and sugar. Add all remaining ingredients including date mixture. Beat 2 minutes. Spread in a 20cm (8in) baking dish. Microwave on 50% power for 6 minutes and HIGH 2–5 minutes. Cover with greaseproof paper. Let stand directly on oven top 10 minutes. Frost with Orange Fluff Frosting (page 134) or serve with whipped cream.

Hummingbird Cake
A yummy cake!

Makes one 22.5cm (9in) layer

75g (3oz) flour
150g (6oz) sugar
1 × 5ml tsp (1tsp) each, baking
  powder and cinnamon
1 × 2.5ml tsp (½tsp) bicarbonate
  of soda
2 eggs

100ml (4fl oz) cooking oil
1 banana, chopped
50g (2oz) walnuts, chopped
3 × 15ml tbsp (3tbsp) crushed
  canned pineapple with juice
Few drops vanilla essence

Place all ingredients in mixing bowl. Blend at low speed, then at medium speed 2 minutes. Spread batter in a 22.5cm (9in) round dish. Microwave on 50% power for 6 minutes and HIGH 2–6 minutes until done. Cover with greaseproof paper and let stand directly on oven top 5–10 minutes. Cool and frost with Cream Cheese Frosting. See page 134.

🐦 The cake top can be soft and sticky. To dry the surface and help the frosting stick to the cake, sprinkle about 1 × 15ml tbsp (1tbsp) biscuit crumbs or granulated sugar on each layer after baking and before frosting.

Crumb Cake

Makes one 22.5cm (9in) square

100g (4oz) sugar
50g (2oz) butter
2 eggs
1 × 5ml tsp (1tsp) baking powder
100g (4oz) digestive biscuits,
    crushed

25g (1oz) flour
100ml (4fl oz) milk
50g (2oz) chopped nuts
Fewe drops vanilla essence

Mix together baking powder and biscuit crumbs. Cream butter and sugar. Add eggs and vanilla. Add dry ingredients alternately with milk. Stir in nuts. Pour into greased 20cm (8in) square dish. Shield corners with foil, if oven permits. Microwave on HIGH 5–6 minutes. Cover with clingfilm and let stand 10 minutes on oven top. Spread topping on while cake is hot.

Topping: Combine 100g (4oz) crushed pineapple, drained and 100g (4oz) sugar. Microwave on HIGH until clear.

Pineapple Cake

Makes two 20cm (8in) squares

100g (4oz) butter
225g (8oz) sugar
2 eggs
Few drops vanilla essence
1 × 566g (20oz) can crushed
    pineapple, in heavy syrup,
    undrained

225g (8oz) flour
1 × 5ml tsp (1tsp) bicarbonate of
    soda
1 × 2.5ml tsp (½tsp) salt
1 × 7.5ml tsp (1½tsp) baking
    powder

Cream butter and sugar. Add eggs, vanilla and pineapple. Sift dry ingredients together and stir into the sugar mixture. Spread in two 20cm (8in) square dishes. Shield corners. Microwave one at a time on 50% power for 6 minutes and HIGH 2–6 minutes until done. Let stand directly on oven top 5–10 minutes. While cake is standing prepare frosting and frost cake while hot.

Frosting: Cream 450g (1lb) sifted icing sugar and 225g (8oz) of cream cheese. (The cheese may be microwaved on HIGH about 45 seconds to soften.) Add 50–100g (2–4oz) chopped nuts. Spread on cake.

Chocolate Cake

Makes a 22.5cm (9in) square

100g (4oz) flour
225g (8oz) sugar
1 × 1.25ml tsp (¼tsp) salt
50ml (2fl oz) oil
50g (2oz) butter
40g (1½oz) cocoa

75ml (3fl oz) water
50ml (2fl oz) buttermilk
1 × 2.5ml tsp (½tsp) each
bicarbonate of soda and vanilla
essence
1 egg

Combine flour, sugar and salt. Combine water, oil, butter and cocoa and microwave on HIGH 3 to 4 minutes to boiling. Pour over dry ingredients and mix. Add remaining ingredients, beating well. Pour into 22.5cm (9in) square dish. Shield corners with foil, if oven permits. Microwave on 50% power 6 minutes and HIGH 2–6 minutes till done. Let stand directly on oven top 5–10 minutes. While cake is standing prepare frosting and frost cake while hot.

Frosting:

50g (2oz) butter
2 × 15ml tbsp (2tbsp) cocoa
3 × 15ml tbsp (3tbsp) milk

225g (½lb) icing sugar
50g (2oz) chopped nuts
Few drops of vanilla essence

Combine butter, cocoa, milk and vanilla essence and microwave on HIGH 2–3 minutes until it boils. Add icing sugar and beat. Add nuts and spread on hot cake.

🐦 Fruit cakes will require longer baking time than other cakes since they are more dense.

🐦 To make a torte, freeze the cake, split each layer horizontally and frost.

🐦 Clear glass baking dishes enable you to check the bottom for uncooked batter.

Quick Cake
As quick as a mix!

Makes one 20cm (8in) layer
100g (4oz) butter
175g (7oz) flour
225g (8oz) sugar
2 × 5ml tsp (2tsp) baking powder

1 × 2.5ml tsp (½tsp) salt
1 egg
150ml (6fl oz) milk
Few drops vanilla essence

Beat all ingredients together and pour into a 20cm (8in) dish. Microwave on 50% power for 6 minutes and HIGH 2–5 minutes. Let stand directly on oven top to cool.

Cupcakes: Cupcakes are especially easy and quick to microwave and fun for 'very young cooks'. For best results always use 2 paper liners in each cup to absorb excess moisture. The cupcakes cook so fast that moisture pulled out of the batter does not have time to evaporate. The two layers of paper absorb some of the moisture so that the cupcakes are not soggy. Fill ⅓ to ½ full with batter. If using ramekins, arrange them in a circular pattern in the oven. After cooking, remove the cupcakes from custard cups or baking dish as soon as they are done. Let cool on a rack 2–3 minutes. Since cake doesn't brown, use frosting, crumb, nut or spice toppings for eye appeal. Use these cooking times as a guide.

Quantity	HIGH POWER
1	25–30 seconds
2	¾–1¼ minutes
3	1–1½ minutes
4	1½–2 minutes
5	2–2½ minutes
6	2–3 minutes

🐄 If your oven requires rotating food for even cooking, simplify turning cupcakes by placing them on a microwave-safe plate or tray. The plate can be rotated instead of having to reposition each cupcake.

Fruit Cake

Makes one 22.5cm (9in) layer

175g (7oz) brown sugar
1 egg
150g (6oz) flour
1 × 2.5ml tsp (½tsp) salt
1 × 5ml tsp (1tsp) each
    bicarbonate of soda and
    cinnamon
325g (12oz) fresh or frozen fruit.
    Consistency of batter varies with
    fruit used. If mixture is too dry,
    several 15ml tbsp (tbsp) of milk
    may be added.

Topping:
40g (1½oz) brown sugar
50g (2oz) nuts, chopped
25g (1oz) flour
1 × 2.5ml tsp (½tsp) cinnamon
50g (2oz) butter

Beat all cake ingredients except fruit together. Fold in fruit. Spread in 22.5cm (9in) dish. Combine topping ingredients and sprinkle on batter. Microwave on 50% power for 6 minutes and on HIGH 2-6 minutes or until done.

Italian Cream Cake

Makes one 22.5cm (9in) layer

100g (4oz) butter
150g (6oz) sugar
75g (3oz) flour
1 × 2.5ml tsp (½tsp) bicarbonate
    of soda
2 eggs

1 × 5ml tsp (1tsp) baking powder
25g (1oz) coconut
50g (2oz) chopped nuts
100ml (4fl oz) buttermilk
Few drops vanilla essence

Cream butter and sugar. Add eggs. Combine dry ingredients and add to butter mixture alternately with buttermilk. Fold in coconut and nuts. Add vanilla. Spread in a 22.5cm (9in) square dish and microwave on 50% power for 6 minutes and HIGH 2–6 minutes, or until done. Frost with Cream Cheese Nut Frosting. See page 134.

Shortcake
*Simply scrumptious when served with fresh fruits
and whipped cream!*

150g (6oz) flour
1 × 5ml tsp (1tsp) baking powder
Pinch salt
6 × 15ml tbsp (6tbsp) sugar
50g (2oz) butter

1 egg
1½ × 15ml tbsp (1½tbsp) cognac
1 × 15ml tbsp (1 tbsp) grated
lemon or orange rind

Sift flour, baking powder and salt together. Add sugar and butter, and work with fingers till smooth. Add egg and cognac and work into mixture. Add citrus rind. Shape dough into a ball. Flatten to about a 20cm (8in) circle. Brush with beaten egg and score with fork. Microwave on 50% power for 5 minutes and HIGH 3–4 minutes. If possible, let mellow at room temperature overnight. (To make egg wash, combine 1 egg and 2 × 15ml tbsp (2tbsp) water.)

🍴 For a browned shortcake, put under the conventional grill for a few minutes.

Cake Fillings

Cake fillings are basically thick sweet sauces. See 'sauces' in the Desserts chapter for additional filling ideas. To use a sauce recipe as a cake filling, add a little more thickening or cook to a thicker consistency. Cool before spreading on cake. Also see 'puddings'.

Lemon Cheese Filling

6 egg yolks
325g (12oz) sugar

100g (4oz) butter
4 lemons, juice and grated rind

Combine ingredients and microwave on HIGH 5–8 minutes or until thickened, stirring several times.

Coconut Filling

1 × 368g (13oz) can evaporated
  milk
225g (8oz) sugar
100g (4oz) butter
3 × 15ml tbsp (3tbsp) flour

Few drops vanilla essence
75g (3oz) desiccated coconut
50g (2oz) chopped pecans or
  walnuts (optional)

Combine milk, sugar, butter, flour and vanilla together in a deep bowl. Microwave on 50%–70% power until thickened, about 5–10 minutes. Stir several times during cooking. Stir in coconut and nuts. Cool completely before using.

Chocolate Filling

275g (10oz) sugar
1 × 1.25ml tsp (¼tsp) cream of
  tartar
150ml (6fl oz) water
8 egg yolks

40g (1½oz) dark cocoa
Few drops vanilla essence
450g (1lb) butter

Combine sugar, cream of tartar and water and microwave on HIGH until just boiling 116°C (240°F). Meanwhile, beat egg yolks 3–4 minutes. Pour hot syrup into eggs in a slow steady stream while continuing to beat. Continue beating 10–15 minutes until smooth thick cream. Beat in cocoa and vanilla. Then beat in butter a tbsp at a time. Refrigerate until ready to use.

Instant Chocolate Frosting

1 × 397g (14oz) can sweetened
  condensed milk

150g (6oz) broken chocolate or
  chocolate buttons

Microwave on 70% power 2–3 minutes. Stir until chocolate melts. Heat a few more seconds if needed to make a smooth mixture. Good especially on chocolate cake.

🐾 Toasted coconut. Spread 50g (2oz) desiccated coconut on a pie plate and microwave uncovered on HIGH for about 1 minute. Stir and cook 1 minute longer.

Caramel Icing

675g (1½lb) sugar
150ml (6fl oz) evaporated milk

225g (8oz) butter

Combine 450g (1lb) sugar, milk, and butter in a deep bowl and microwave at 70% power about 5–6 minutes to dissolve sugar and melt butter. In a separate dish, combine remaining sugar and 1 × 15ml tbsp (1tbsp) water. Microwave on HIGH 3–6 minutes or until sugar caramelizes (becomes brown and liquid). Watch carefully after first 2 minutes of cooking. Add caramelized sugar to the first mixture and microwave on 70% power for 15–20 minutes or until mixture reaches about 110°C (225°F), very soft ball stage. Cool a few minutes and beat with electric mixer until thickened and smooth. Add chopped nuts if desired.

Crème au Beurre
A rich, delicious buttercream filling

225g (8oz) sugar
75ml (3fl oz) hot water
1 × 1.25ml tsp (¼tsp) cream of
tartar

8 egg yolks
225g (8oz) butter

Microwave sugar, water and cream of tartar on HIGH to soft-ball stage 116°C (240°F) about 5–10 minutes. Meanwhile, beat egg yolks until light and fluffy. Pour syrup very gradually into the egg yolks, beating constantly. Continue beating until the mixture is cool and very thick and fluffy. Add softened butter, a little at a time, continuing to beat.

🐦 To vary the flavour of Crème Au Beurre, beat in 3 × 15ml tbsp (3tbsp) cognac, rum, liqueur or fruit purée after butter has been added.

🐦 To reheat individual portions of frosted or unfrosted cake, place each piece on a plate. Cover with greaseproof paper. Microwave on HIGH 10–15 seconds or until heated.

Cream Cheese Frosting

Makes icing for 1 layer

100g (4oz) softened cream cheese
40g (1½oz) softened butter

225g (½lb) icing sugar
Few drops vanilla essence

Blend ingredients and beat until light and fluffy. Thin with a little milk or cream, if desired.

Cream Cheese Nut Frosting: Add 50g (2oz) chopped nuts to Cream Cheese Frosting.

Five-minute Frosting

Frosts two 22.5cm (9in) layers

225g (8oz) sugar
100ml (4fl oz) water
1 × 1.25ml tsp (¼tsp) cream of
   tartar

Pinch of salt
2 egg whites
Few drops of vanilla essence

Combine sugar, water, cream of tartar and salt in deep bowl. Microwave on 70% power for 4–5 minutes or until mixture boils. Meanwhile, beat egg whites until soft peaks form. Gradually pour in hot syrup, beat about 5 minutes or until thick and fluffy. Blend in vanilla.

Variations:

Seafoam Frosting: Substitute light brown sugar for white. It's Simply Scrumptious on spice or apple cake.

Pineapple: Substitute pineapple juice for water. Fold in 2 × 5ml tsp (2tsp) grated lemon rind.

Pink Cloud: Fold in 50g (2oz) well drained, finely chopped maraschino cherries.

Lemon: Decrease water 1 × 15ml tbsp (1tbsp) and add 3 × 15ml tbsp (3tbsp) lemon juice. After beating, fold in 1 × 5ml tsp (1tsp) lemon rind and 1 × 2.5ml tsp (½tsp) almond extract.

Chocolate: Fold in 25g (1oz) plain bitter chocolate melted. (Microwave at 70% power 2–3 minutes.)

Marshmallow: Fold in 6–8 marshmallows, quartered.

Orange Fluff: Substitute orange juice for water. Fold in 2 × 5ml tsp (2tsp) grated orange rind (optional). Delicious on Date Nut Party Cake (see page 126).

Best Ever Chocolate Icing

675g (1½lb) sugar
50g (2oz) cocoa

150ml (6fl oz) evaporated milk
150g (6oz) butter

Combine ingredients in a deep bowl and microwave on 70% power about 5–10 minutes or until mixture starts to thicken. Let cool at room temperature until luke warm. Beat to spreading consistency.

Buttercream Frosting

Icing for two 20cm (8in) layers
225g (8oz) icing sugar
Few drops vanilla essence
40g (1½oz) butter

1–2 × 15ml tbsp (1–2tbsp) double cream

Microwave butter and cream on 50% power for 1–2 minutes or until bubbling. Add sugar and vanilla and beat until smooth. Add a few drops cream if needed to achieve spreading consistency.

Variations:

Fudge: Add 50g (2oz) plain bitter chocolate to butter and cream. Microwave on 50% power 3–4 minutes to melt chocolate.

Coffee: Add 1 × 2.5ml tsp (½tsp) instant coffee to butter before microwaving.

Lemon: Substitute 1 × 15ml tbsp (1tbsp) lemon juice and 1 × 15ml tbsp (1tbsp) cream for cream. Add 1 × 15ml tbsp (1tbsp) grated lemon peel and 2–3 drops yellow food colouring.

Orange: Substitute orange juice for cream and add 1 × 5ml tsp (1tsp) grated orange rind.

Peanut Butter Frosting: Add 2 × 5ml tsp (2tsp) peanut butter to butter before microwaving.

Butterscotch: Add 50g (2oz) brown sugar to butter before microwaving and cook an additional minute or two to dissolve sugar.

🐾 Leftover toppings and icings may be refrigerated. Make them 'spreadable' by microwaving a few seconds.

Japanese Fruit Cake Filling

675g (1½lb) sugar
325ml (12fl oz) water
6 × 15ml tbsp (6tbsp) cornflour
Juice of 2 lemons

75–100g (3–4oz) fresh grated
   coconut
Rind of 1 lemon

Combine sugar, water and juice with cornflour; microwave for 4–6 minutes until thickened. Cool and add coconut and rind.

Pineapple Cake Filling

6 × 15ml tbsp (6tbsp) crushed
   pineapple
150g (6oz) sugar

3 × 15ml tbsp (3tbsp) flour
25g (1oz) butter

Melt butter for 30 seconds on HIGH. Add flour and stir to blend. Add crushed pineapple and sugar and microwave for 3–4 minutes until thick, stirring midway during cooking time.

Apricot-Pineapple Filling

6 × 15ml tbsp (6tbsp) crushed
   pineapple
100g (4oz) crushed dried apricots

100g (4oz) sugar
3 × 15ml tbsp (3tbsp) orange juice
75g (3oz) flaked coconut

Combine pineapple, apricots, sugar and orange juice in a measuring jug. Cook for 4–5 minutes on HIGH, stirring several times. Remove from oven and cover with clingfilm. Allow to stand 5 minutes. Add coconut and spread over a 20cm (8in) cake while still warm. Garnish with whipped cream.

🍴 Opening the oven door will not cause the cake to 'fall' as it sometimes does conventionally since there is no heat in the microwave oven.

🍴 Microwaved cakes are very soft. You may prefer to slightly freeze the cake layers before you split them.

Simply Scrumptious
Pies and Desserts

General Guidelines

Fruit-pie fillings have a Simply Scrumptious fresh flavour and texture because of their short cooking time. Cream fillings are simple to prepare since they do not have to be constantly stirred to prevent scorching as in conventional cooking. Conventional recipes usually need no ingredient changes for microwave use.

Pastry crusts. Always prebake the pie shell. To minimise pie-crust shrinkage during microwaving, allow dough to rest 3–5 minutes before final shaping and do not stretch dough while putting into pie plate.

Allow crust to cool before adding fillings. Crusts become crisper during cooling. Check that the crust is cooked a minute before minimum suggested cooking time, since crusts differ in thickness and moisture content. Pastry should be dry and opaque when done.

Double-crust pies cannot be microwaved because the crust will not cook properly. There is too much steam and moisture from the filling for the upper crust to be dry and crisp. To give fruit pies the appearance of a top crust, use lattice or pastry cut-outs that have been microwaved separately. Crumb crusts adapt to microwaving without change in ingredients. Use less filling since it bubbles hard. A high-fluted pastry edge helps contain the bubbling filling. Use a reduced power setting, 50% or 70%, to stop mixture from boiling over.

Wholewheat Pastry

25g (1oz) lard
50g (2oz) butter or margarine
150g (6oz) wholewheat plain flour
1 × 2.5ml tsp (½tsp) salt

3 × 15ml tbsp (3tbsp) cold water
1 × 15ml tbsp (1tbsp) brown sugar
(optional)

Cut lard and butter or margarine into flour and salt with pastry blender until mixture forms coarse crumbs. Add sugar if desired. Sprinkle water over mixture while stirring with a fork until mixture is moist enough to cling together (you may not need all the water). Place in a 22.5cm (9in) pie plate and let rest 10 minutes to reduce shrinkage. Trim and crimp edges. Prick crust with fork. Microwave on HIGH 5–7 minutes. When done, crust will appear dry and opaque.

Biscuit Crust

Makes 22.5cm (9in) pie shell
100g (4oz) butter
225g (8oz) digestive biscuits,
　crushed

2 × 15ml tbsp (2tbsp) brown sugar
(optional)

Microwave butter in pie plate on HIGH 45–60 seconds. Stir in crumbs and sugar. Press mixture against bottom and side of plate. Microwave on HIGH 1½ minutes. Cool.

🐦 Use wholewheat pastry for cream, mincemeat, apple, peach and other fruit pies.

Oatmeal Crust

150g (6oz) quick-cooking oats   100g (4oz) butter
75g (3oz) soft brown sugar   25g (1oz) plain flour

Combine oats, butter, sugar and flour and press firmly against bottom and sides of 22.5cm (9in) pie plate. If possible, place a 20cm (8in) pie plate on top of crumb mixture and press down. Microwave on HIGH 2–3 minutes. Press crust again against pie plate. Stand 5–10 minutes. Very good with chocolate pie filling (page 149).

Other Simply Scrumptious crusts

Pecan Crust: 100g (4oz) flour, 2 × 15ml tbsp (2tbsp) brown sugar, 100g (4oz) butter, 50g (2oz) chopped pecans. Mix ingredients together until particles resemble coarse crumbs. Press on bottom and sides of a 22.5cm (9in) pie plate. Microwave on HIGH 3–5minutes.

Chocolate Coconut Crust: 50g (2oz) plain chocolate, 25g (1oz) butter, 2 × 15ml tbsp (2tbsp) hot milk, 50g (2oz) sifted icing sugar, 100g (4oz) thin-flaked coconut, toasted or untoasted. Melt chocolate and butter by microwaving on 70% power 3–4 minutes. Add milk and sugar, stirring well. Add coconut. Spread in bottom and sides of buttered 22.5cm (9in) pie plate. Chill until firm. (Do not freeze.) Fill with cream pie filling or softened ice cream.

Chocolate Fondue

25g (1oz) chocolate   2 × 15ml tbsp (2tbsp) dark rum
100ml (4fl oz) whipping cream

Cook all ingredients on HIGH about 2–2½ minutes until melted and very hot. Stir several times. Use fresh fruit – pineapple, apple, orange, strawberries, grapes, bananas – or sponge cake, cut into cubes for dipping.

To reheat, microwave on 50% power 30–45 seconds.

🐓 Substitute cereal crumbs, gingersnaps or chocolate wheatmeal biscuits for digestive biscuits.

Banana-split Dessert

Base:
225g (8oz) digestive biscuits, crushed
100g (4oz) butter

Filling:
375ml (¾pt) cooled thick custard

Topping:
3 large bananas
560g (20oz) can crushed pineapple, drained
75g (3oz) chopped nuts
75g (3oz) glacé cherries, diced
250ml (½pt) whipping cream, whipped

Prepare base by melting butter on HIGH about 1 minute and stirring into biscuit crumbs. Press mixture into a 25cm × 35cm (10 × 14in) dish.

Pour filling over crust and chill till set.

Topping: Cover filling with sliced bananas, then carefully spread on crushed pineapple, whipped cream and sprinkle on nuts and cherries. Refrigerate.

Butterscotch and Date Pie

Pastry case or crumb crust
400ml (16fl oz) evaporated milk
75g (3oz) butter
4 egg yolks
150g (6oz) light brown sugar
3 × 15ml tbsp (3tbsp) cornflour
2 × 15ml tbsp (2tbsp) plain flour
Pinch of salt
75g (3oz) chopped dates
Few drops vanilla essence

Whipped cream and nuts to garnish

Heat milk and butter on HIGH 5 minutes. Combine sugar, cornflour, plain flour, and salt; beat in egg yolks; then add to heated milk. Cook until thick, about 4–6 minutes on HIGH. Stir in dates and vanilla. Chill and pour into pie shell. Just before serving, garnish with whipped cream and sprinkle nuts on top.

♨ To crisp and renew the fresh flavour of day-old cookies microwave uncovered on HIGH 5–15 seconds.

Pecan Cream Cheese Pie

Crust:
225g (8oz) digestive biscuits,
    crushed
100g (4oz) butter
50g (2oz) finely chopped pecans or
    walnuts

Filling:
450g (1lb) cream cheese
225g (8oz) brown sugar
100g (4oz) chopped pecans or
    walnuts

Topping:
225ml (8fl oz) sour cream
2 × 15ml tbsp (2tbsp) brown sugar
Few drops vanilla essence

Combine crust ingredients and press into a 22.5cm (9in) pie plate. Cook on HIGH 1½ minutes. Microwave cream cheese on HIGH about 45 seconds to soften; beat in sugar until smooth and creamy. Add nuts and spoon into base. Cook on 50% power about 5 minutes. Mix topping ingredients and spoon over pie. Microwave on 50% power for 3 minutes. Cool and garnish with chopped pecans or walnuts. Chill.

Chocomint Dessert
A good dessert for a crowd

Serves 16

Crust:
225g (8oz) finely crushed
    chocolate digestive biscuits
100g (4oz) butter

Chocolate Pie Filling:
    Recipe on page 149
Peppermint flavouring to taste

Green filling:
1 × 365g (13oz) can evaporated
    milk
1 × 135g (5oz) packet
    lime-flavoured jelly
225g (8oz) cream cheese
225g (8oz) sugar
Several drops green food colouring

Prepare crust by microwaving butter on HIGH about 45 seconds to melt. Combine the crumbs; reserve 3 × 15ml tbsp (3tbsp) for topping. Press remainder over bottom of 22.5cm × 32cm (9 × 13in) dish.

To prepare the green filling, freeze evaporated milk in freezer tray until crystals form around the edges. Meanwhile, microwave 225ml (8fl oz) water for 2–2½ minutes to boiling. Dissolve jelly in water and let stand 30 minutes. Beat together cream cheese and sugar; gradually beat in jelly and food colouring. Whip evaporated milk to soft peaks; fold in cheese mixture. Spread half over crust; chill 1 hour. Keep remaining mixture at room temperature. Make chocolate pie filling and stir in flavouring. Cool. Spoon over green layer. Top with remaining cheese mixture. Sprinkle with crumbs. Chill.

White Chocolate Mousse
Simply Scrumptious with fresh strawberries!

Serves 8 to 10
275g (10oz) white chocolate
100g (4oz) sugar
50ml (2fl oz) water
4 egg whites
Few drops vanilla essence
2 × 15ml tbsp (2tbsp) Cointreau
225ml (8fl oz) double cream

Break chocolate into small pieces. Microwave at 70% for 2–3 minutes or until chocolate melts. Prepare syrup by microwaving the sugar and water until soft ball stage, 112°C (230°F), about 5–10 minutes at 70%. Meanwhile, beat egg whites until soft peaks form. Pour in syrup while beating and continue beating until mixture is room temperature (Italian meringue). Fold in chocolate, cointreau and vanilla. Whip cream and fold into chocolate mixture. Freeze. Serve garnished with chocolate curls or fresh fruit.

🌶 A Simply Scrumptious quick crust may be made by substituting shortbread crumbs for digestive biscuits to make a crust for fruit filling or other filling you would ordinarily put in a pastry case.

Ice Cream Bombe

A bombe is a combination of 2 or more flavours of ice cream or sorbet usually formed in a round mould or bowl. Microwave simplifies and hastens the preparation of a bombe since the ice cream can be softened to the proper consistency in seconds. They are 'easy and elegant' and can be made days in advance.

To prepare the mould or bowl, oil lightly and line with clingfilm, smoothing out all wrinkles. Chill thoroughly.

Each layer must be put into the mould when soft enough to be spread (but not too soft) then frozen hard before the next layer is added.

Hard ice cream may be softened at 40% power. Allow 15–30 seconds for 500ml (1pt), 30–45 seconds for 1 litre (1¾pt).

Elegant Bombe

Serves 8 to 10
This is a favourite. It has 4 layers: chocolate, vanilla, raspberry and ganache cream (fudge).

First layer: 1 litre (1¾pt) good quality chocolate ice cream. Press in a 2 litre (3½pt) bowl or mould. This will make about a 1.8cm (¾in) layer covering the inside surface of the bowl. Smooth with the back side of a wet spoon. Freeze.

Second layer: 1 litre (1¾pt) good quality vanilla ice cream. Add a 1.8cm (¾in) layer of vanilla ice cream over the chocolate. Smooth and freeze.

Third layer: 1 litre (1¾pt) raspberry frozen yogurt. Smooth over vanilla layer. Freeze.

Fourth layer: Ganache Cream (recipe follows). Spoon on top of raspberry layer to fill cavity. Level the top. Freeze at least 2 hours, preferably longer. Let bombe mellow in refrigerator about 30 minutes before serving. Unmould and decorate with whipped cream, if desired. Slice in wedges to serve.

Ganache Cream: 100ml (4fl oz) double cream, 100g (4oz) chocolate, pinch salt, 1 × 5ml tsp (1tsp) powdered instant coffee. Microwave half the cream, chocolate, salt and coffee on 70%

power for about 1–2 minutes, or until chocolate melts, stirring several times. Do not boil. Stir until very smooth. Cool to room temperature. Whip remaining cream and gently fold into chocolate mixture. Chill. Ganache may also be used as a cake filling, or thinned with additional coffee and served as a sauce over ice cream.

Steamed Prune Pudding
Delicious Christmas tradition!

Steamed puddings microwave beautifully. The appearance is the same as conventionally baked. Microwave cooking time: about 15 minutes. Conventional cooking time: 2 hours.

Serves 8

125g (5oz) sifted flour
1 × 2.5ml tsp (½tsp) salt
1 × 5ml tsp (1tsp) bicarbonate of soda
65g (2½oz) butter
225g (8oz) firmly packed brown sugar

3 eggs
225g (8oz) pitted prunes
2 × 15ml tbsp (2tbsp) milk
50ml (2fl oz) vegetable oil
Caster sugar

Add boiling water to cover prunes, cover with clingfilm and microwave on HIGH 5 minutes. Let prunes sit until plumped, then drain. Sift flour, salt and bicarbonate of soda together. Beat butter, sugar and eggs thoroughly. Add prunes. Blend in dry ingredients. Add milk and oil. Avoid overmixing. Prepare a 1.4 litre (2½pt) ring mould or other heatproof ceramic mould by greasing well and dusting with biscuit crumbs. Spread batter in mould, cover tightly with clingfilm, securing around the dish with rubber band. Sit mould on an inverted pie plate in the oven; microwave on 50% power for 13 minutes and HIGH 2–8 minutes or until done. Cool covered on a heatproof surface 10 minutes. Invert; dust with caster sugar. Serve with hard sauce or whipped cream.

Hard sauce. 100g (4oz) butter, 450g (1lb) caster sugar, 2 × 15ml tbsp (2tbsp) brandy. Beat butter until fluffy. Mix in remaining ingredients.

Lemon Meringue Pie

375g (14oz) sugar
50g (2oz) cornflour
1 × 1.25ml tsp (¼tsp) salt
250ml (½pt) water
3 eggs, separated

100ml (4fl oz) lemon juice
2 × 5ml tsp (2tsp) lemon rind,
  grated
25g (1oz) butter
Baked pie crust or biscuit crust

Reserve 6 × 15ml tbsp (6tbsp) sugar for meringue. Mix together the remaining sugar, cornflour, water and salt. Microwave on HIGH 4–6 minutes or until mixture is transparent, stirring after mixture cooks 2 minutes. Beat egg yolks and lemon juice together, adding 100ml (4fl oz) of the hot mixture. Mix well and add to hot cornflour mixture. Cook 4–6 minutes on 70% power, stirring several times until thickened. Add rind and butter. Mix well. To prevent film from forming on filling, place clingfilm directly on surface while it cools.

Prepare meringue by beating egg whites and a pinch of salt until soft peaks form. Gradually add reserved sugar, continuing to beat until stiff. Pile meringue on top of filling, spreading to edges to prevent shrinking. Microwave on HIGH 2–3 minutes. Meringue will be light and firm, but not brown. To brown the meringue, use the conventional oven.

Banana Pudding Cream Filling

325ml (12fl oz) milk or single
  cream
1 egg
2 × 15ml tbsp (2tbsp) cornflour

Pinch of salt
150g (6oz) sugar
Few drops vanilla essence
40g (1½oz) butter

Microwave milk on HIGH for 3–5 minutes or to boiling. Mix sugar, cornflour and egg together. Add about 100ml (4fl oz) of hot milk, stirring to blend. Add to remaining milk and cook for 4–5 minutes on 70% power or until thickened. Add butter, vanilla and salt. Cool.

🍮 To make banana pudding, layer vanilla wafers and banana slices. Pour half of cream filling over bananas and repeat layers.

Cheesecake
Fill the centre with strawberries for a
very impressive dessert

450g (1lb) cream cheese
450g (1lb) creamed cottage cheese
325g (12oz) sugar
4 eggs
2 × 15ml tbsp (2tbsp) cornflour
2 × 15ml tbsp (2tbsp) plain flour

50ml (2fl oz) lemon juice, freshly
 squeezed
1 × 15ml tbsp (1tbsp) grated
 lemon rind
Few drops vanilla essence
75g (3oz) butter, melted
225ml (8fl oz) sour cream

Oil a microwave-safe bundt cake pan and sprinkle with sugar to coat. Soften cream cheese for 2–3 minutes on 30% power. Place in large mixing bowl and beat cream cheese and cottage cheese at high speed until well blended. Gradually add sugar, then eggs, beating well after each addition. Add cornflour, plain flour, lemon juice, rind, and vanilla. Add melted butter and sour cream. Beat only until smooth. Pour into bundt pan and microwave for 18 minutes on 50% power, and 3–6 minutes on HIGH. Let stand in pan for 2 hours. Then remove and let cool before placing in refrigerator. Chill at least 3 hours before serving. Garnish with fresh strawberries or other fruit. Freezes well.

Japanese Fruit Pie

100g (4oz) butter
150g (6oz) sugar
3 eggs
50g (2oz) desiccated coconut

50g (2oz) pecans
75g (3oz) chocolate, broken into
 small pieces
23cm (9in) baked pastry case

Microwave butter and chocolate in a deep bowl on 70% power for about 2 minutes. Stir to melt. Stir in pecans, coconut, sugar and eggs. Pour filling into baked pastry case and microwave on 50% power about 8 minutes. Stir once, very gently, during cooking. Cool before serving.

🖐 Soften ice cream or melt a slice of cheese on apple pie in 15–20 seconds per piece on HIGH.

Chocolate Pecan Pie

Crust:
150g (6oz) ground pecans
1 egg, separated
50g (2oz) sugar
1 × 15ml tbsp (1tbsp) cocoa

Filling:
150g (6oz) chocolate, broken into
   small pieces
1 egg, separated
Few drops vanilla essence
250ml (½pt) double cream,
   whipped

Make crust: Beat egg white until stiff (reserve yolk for filling). Gradually add sugar, beating until stiff and glossy; beat in cocoa. Fold in ground nuts. Press mixture firmly onto bottom and sides of well buttered 22.5cm (9in) pie plate. Microwave on HIGH 3–6 minutes.

Prepare filling: Melt chocolate on 70% power for 2–4 minutes. Stir in 2 egg yolks and vanilla; set aside to cool. Beat remaining egg white until stiff; set aside. Whip cream: Fold half of cream into chocolate mixture. Then fold in beaten egg white. Pile into pie crust; decorate with remaining whipped cream and chocolate curls. Chill.

Quick Fruit Cobbler
Terrific winter dessert!

100g (4oz) butter
225ml (8fl oz) milk
10g (4oz) self-raising flour

225g (8oz) sugar
750ml (1½pt) fruit (sweetened to
   taste)

Microwave butter on HIGH 1 minute to melt in a 2 litre (3½pt) casserole. Add milk, flour and sugar and mix together. Pour fruit over batter; do not stir. Microwave on HIGH 8–10 minutes or until done. If you want to brown the crust, sprinkle with sugar and cinnamon and place under the conventional grill a few minutes. Serve with whipped cream, ice cream or a rum or vanilla sauce.

♡ **Black Cherry Pudding:** Quick Fruit Cobbler, substituting a 400g (16oz) can sweet black cherries, drained and chopped and 100g (4oz) chopped pecans or walnuts for the fruit.

Pineapple-Lemon Pie

Crust:
150g (6oz) sifted plain flour
50g (2oz) sugar
1 × 5ml tsp (1tsp) grated lemon
peel
150g (6oz) butter
25g (1oz) oats
2 egg yolks

Filling:
225g (8oz) sugar
25g (1oz) cornflour
Pinch of salt

225ml (8fl oz) water
1 × 225g (8oz) can crushed
pineapple
4 egg yolks, slightly beaten
1 × 5ml tsp (1tsp) grated lemon
peel
50ml (2fl oz) lemon juice
1 × 15ml tbsp (1tbsp) butter
3 × 15ml tbsp (3tbsp) kirsch or
rum (optional)
225ml (8fl oz) whipping cream,
whipped

Prepare crust: Sift flour and sugar. Add peel. Rub in butter until mixture resembles coarse crumbs. Stir in oats. Add egg yolks. Knead lightly. Microwave in a 22.5cm (9in) pie plate on HIGH 5–7 minutes.

Filling: Combine sugar, cornflour and salt. Stir in water and pineapple. Microwave on HIGH 6–8 minutes, or until thickened and clear, stirring several times. Add egg yolks, blending a little of the hot mixture into the eggs first. Microwave on HIGH 1 minute. Stir in peel, juice, butter and kirsch. Cool slightly and pour into pie shell. Decorate with whipped cream and lemon curls.

Kahlua Pie

Crust:
100g (4oz) butter
225g (8oz) digestive biscuits,
crushed

Filling:
1 litre (1¾pt) coffee ice cream
Kahlua liqueur
225ml (8fl oz) whipping cream,
whipped

Microwave butter in 22.5cm (9in) pie plate on HIGH ½–1 minute to melt. Mix in biscuit crumbs. Press against bottom and sides of plate. Microwave on HIGH 2–3 minutes. Cool. Fill pie shell with ice cream. Pour Kahlua over ice cream. Top with whipped cream.

Rum Cream Pie
Simply Scrumptious! Good, light Christmas dessert

Crust:
225g (8oz) digestive biscuits,
    crushed
100g (4oz) butter, melted
2 × 15ml tbsp (2tbsp) sugar
1 × 2.5ml tsp (½tsp) ground
    cinnamon
50g (2oz) chopped pecans

Filling:
1 × 15g (½oz) sachet gelatine
100ml (4fl oz) cold water
5 egg yolks
225g (8oz) sugar
50ml (2fl oz) dark rum
250ml (½pt) whipping cream,
    whipped
Grated chocolate to decorate

Combine crust ingredients and press in a 22.5cm (9in) pie plate. Microwave on HIGH 3 minutes. Chill. Soften gelatine in water. Microwave on HIGH 45 seconds–1 minute to dissolve gelatine. Beat egg yolks and sugar until very light. Stir gelatine into egg mixture. Cool. Gradually add rum, beating constantly. Fold whipped cream into egg mixture. Cool until mixture begins to set, then spoon into crust. Chill until firm. Top with grated chocolate.

Chocolate Pie

Serves 8
Oatmeal pie crust
225g (8oz) sugar
3 egg yolks
3 × 15ml tbsp (3tbsp) each: flour,
    cocoa and butter
Few drops vanilla essence
1 × 365g (13oz) can evaporated
    milk

Combine sugar, cocoa, flour and milk. Microwave on HIGH 1½ minutes. Beat egg yolks and add to mixture. Microwave on HIGH 3–6 minutes or until thickened. Stir in butter and vanilla. Pour into cooked crust. Chill and serve with whipped cream – a must!

 Try substituting other liquors or liqueurs for the rum.

Heavenly Chocolate Dessert

Make three different Simply Scrumptious desserts with one basic recipe. Each variation is equally good. Try them all!

Serves 15 to 20
First layer:
100g (4oz) flour   100g (4oz) butter
100g (4oz) chopped pecans

Mix and press into 22.5 × 32.5cm (9 × 13in) dish. Cook at 70% for 4–6 minutes. Cool.

Second layer:
225g (8oz) cream cheese   225ml (8fl oz) whipped cream
225g (8oz) caster sugar

Soften cream cheese on HIGH 45–60 seconds. Stir in sugar. Fold in whipped cream. Spread over crust. Refrigerate 15 minutes.

Third layer:
225g (8oz) sugar   Few drops vanilla essence
3 egg yolks   225ml (8fl oz) evaporated milk
3 × 15ml tbsp (3tbsp) each; flour,
   cocoa and butter

Combine and microwave on HIGH 4–6 minutes or until thickened. Cool and spread over second layer.

Fourth layer:
Top with whipped cream and refrigerate. Garnish with chocolate curls. Cut in squares to serve.

🐄 Chocolate curls. Place unwrapped block of chocolate in microwave and heat 7–10 seconds. Scrape the curls off with a vegetable peeler.

🐄 Marinate bite-sized chunks of fresh pineapple in crème de menthe. Spoon over ice cream or sorbet. Garnish with sugared mint leaves.

Simply Scrumptious Caramel Cream Pie

digestive biscuit pie shell
1 × 397g (14oz) can condensed milk

2 × 15ml tbsp (2tbsp) milk
100ml (4fl oz) whipped cream

Microwave condensed milk in a deep container on 40% power for 12–18 minutes, stirring several times, until the milk caramelises (turns a caramel colour). Stir in 2 × 15ml tbsp (2tbsp) milk to thin; cool completely. Fold in whipped cream and pour into pie shell. Chill. Garnish with whipped cream and nuts if desired.

Simply Scrumptious Strawberry Pie

Serves 8
1.1kg (2½lb) fresh strawberries
225g (8oz) sugar
3 × 15ml tbsp (3tbsp) cornflour
several drops red food colouring
baked pastry case or crumb crust
whipped cream

Purée 450g (1lb) strawberries in blender. Combine sugar and cornflour, stir into puréed strawberries. Microwave on HIGH 2–3 minutes or until it starts to boil. Stir occasionally. Cook on 70% power about 5 minutes or until sauce is smooth and thickened, stirring several times. Add food colouring. Cool. Arrange remaining strawberries in pastry. Spoon cooled sauce over fresh strawberries. Chill and garnish with whipped cream.

🍒 Enjoy hot toppings. Microwave a 311g (11oz) jar of fruit (lid removed) on HIGH for 30–45 seconds, stirring several times.

🍒 Quick Date Nut Cream Pie: Fold 50g (2oz) chopped dates and 50g (2oz) chopped nuts into Caramel Cream before pouring into pie shell.

Scrumptious Apple Pie

450–550g (1–1¼lb) peeled, sliced
  apples
1 × 15ml tbsp (1tbsp) lemon juice
100g (4oz) sugar

50g (2oz) butter
Oatmeal pie crust with ½tsp
  cinnamon added to ingredients
(Pie crust recipe on page 138)

Place apples in a bowl and sprinkle with lemon juice. Cover tightly with clingfilm and microwave on HIGH for 5–7 minutes. Melt butter on HIGH 30 seconds and add sugar stirring to blend. Cook 1 additional minute and add to apples, tossing to coat. Cool slightly and pour in cooled pie crust. Serve warm with whipped cream, ice cream or a slice of cheese.

Austrian Chocolate Mousse

Serves 5 to 6

125g (5oz) plain chocolate, broken
  into small pieces
50g (2oz) butter, softened

4 eggs, separated
1 × 5ml tsp (1tsp) instant coffee

Place chocolate in a deep bowl. Microwave on 70% power 2–4 minutes just until melted. Cool to lukewarm.

Place softened butter, egg yolks, and instant coffee in food processor or mixing bowl and mix thoroughly. Add cooled chocolate, blending well.

Beat egg whites until stiff but not dry. Carefully fold whites into chocolate mixture. Pour into a serving dish or individual glasses. Top with whipped cream to serve.

♥ Cherries Jubilee: 100g (4oz) sugar, 2 × 15ml tbsp (2tbsp) cornflour, pinch of salt, 100ml (4fl oz) red wine, 1 × 616g (22oz) can cherries, 50ml (2fl oz) cognac. Combine sugar, cornflour and salt. Stir in 100ml (4fl oz) water and wine. Add cherries, cover with clingfilm and microwave on HIGH until sauce is thickened, 3–5 minutes. Add cognac. To flame sauce, heat cognac in microwave on HIGH 30–40 seconds or until warm. Gently pour over cherries and ignite. When flame goes out, ladle cherries over ice cream and serve immediately.

Sauces

Enjoy these sauces on ice cream, cream puffs, pancakes, cakes, custards, cheesecake or fruits.

The microwave oven eliminates the possibility of scorching because the cooking occurs from all sides rather than only from the bottom. Continuous stirring is replaced with occasional stirring. Sauces made with cornflour thicken more rapidly and need less stirring than those thickened with flour.

Sauces may be measured, mixed and cooked in the same dish. Use a deep bowl at least 2 to 3 times the volume of the sauce.

Chocolate Sauce I: 375g (14oz) plain chocolate, 225ml (8fl oz) double cream, 2 × 15ml tbsp (2tbsp) cognac or Grand Marnier. Microwave chocolate on 50% power 2–4 minutes to melt. Blend in other ingredients. Makes 275ml (½pt) of rich, delicious sauce for desserts.

Chocolate Sauce II: 450g (1lb) sugar, 25g (1oz) cocoa, 50g (2oz) butter, 1 × 410g (14.5oz) can evaporated milk, a few drops vanilla essence. Combine sugar, cocoa, butter and 100ml (4fl oz) milk and microwave on HIGH 3–5 minutes to dissolve sugar. Add remaining milk and cook on HIGH about 1 minute longer to thicken slightly. Add vanilla. Makes about 675ml (1¼pt).

Caramel Nut Sauce: 325g (12oz) sugar, 175ml (6fl oz) cream, 1 × 15ml tbsp (1tbsp) butter, about 50g (2oz) finely chopped nuts. Mix 100g (4oz) sugar and 1 × 15ml tbsp (1tbsp) water and microwave on HIGH about 4–7 minutes, stirring often until sugar turns light brown. Add remaining sugar and cream and microwave on HIGH until sugar has dissolved. Add butter and beat. Stir in nuts. Makes 325ml (12fl oz).

Strawberry Sauce: 275g (10oz) frozen strawberries, 3 × 15ml tbsp (3tbsp) cornflour, 75g (3oz) sugar, 50ml (2fl oz) water, 1 × 15ml tbsp (1tbsp) lemon juice, few drops red food colouring (optional). Defrost strawberries by microwaving on HIGH 2 minutes. Combine cornflour and juice. Stir in strawberries, microwave on

HIGH 2–5 minutes or until thickened. Stir in lemon juice and colouring.

Cherry Sauce: Melt 175ml (6fl oz) currant jelly on HIGH about 1 minute. Stir in 1 × 825g (1lb 13oz) can pitted cherries, drained. Microwave on HIGH until mixture boils.

Fresh Peach Sauce: 4 fresh peaches, peeled and mashed, 100g (4oz) sugar, 100ml (4fl oz) orange juice, 2 × 5ml tsp (2tsp) lemon juice, few drops vanilla essence. Combine ingredients and microwave on HIGH until thickened.

Orange Sauce: 50g (2oz) butter, 3 × 15ml tbsp (3tbsp) sugar, 3 × 15ml tbsp (3tbsp) Grand Marnier or Cointreau, 225ml (8fl oz) orange juice, 2 × 5ml tsp (2tsp) cornflour, 1 × 2.5ml tsp (½tsp) grated lemon peel, 1 × 2.5ml tsp (½tsp) grated orange peel. Combine butter and sugar, cook on HIGH about 2 minutes. Combine orange juice and cornflour until smooth. Add to butter mixture. Add lemon and orange peel. Cover with clingfilm and cook on HIGH 5 minutes. Add Grand Marnier. Makes 275ml (½pt).

Sweet Cider Sauce: 2 × 15ml tbsp (2tbsp) cornflour, 450ml (16fl oz) sweet apple cider, 3 mashed allspice berries, 1 × 2.5cm (1in) piece cinnamon stick, pinch of salt, dash nutmeg. Place cornflour in a bowl. Gradually whisk in cider until mixture is smooth. Microwave, uncovered on HIGH 4 minutes. Whisk to blend. Stir in spices. Microwave on HIGH 1–1½ minutes until thickened. Strain and serve warm with cake or gingerbread.

Vanilla Custard Sauce: 50g (2oz) sugar, 4 egg yolks, pinch of salt, a few drops of vanilla essence. 450ml (16fl oz) milk. Beat sugar, egg yolks and salt until mixture thickens, 2–3 minutes. Microwave milk with vanilla on HIGH 3–4 minutes just to boiling. Gradually pour hot milk mixture into egg yolk mixture, beating continuously. Microwave on 70% power until mixture thickens. Strain. Serve with fresh fruit or fruit desserts.

Chocolate Syrup: 325g (12oz) sugar, 100g (4oz) cocoa, pinch of salt, 225ml (8fl oz) hot water, a few drops vanilla essence. Mix sugar, cocoa, and salt in a deep bowl. Add 50ml (2fl oz) water, making a smooth paste. Add the remaining 175ml (6fl oz) water. Stir. Microwave on HIGH 1–2 minutes until mixture comes to a boil, stirring several times. Boil 3 minutes. Add vanilla, cool. Makes 425ml (¾pt).

Lemon Whipped Cream Sauce: 225g (8oz) sugar, 100ml (4fl oz) lemon juice, 2 × 15ml tbsp (2tbsp) grated lemon peel, 4 eggs, 225ml (8fl oz) whipping cream, whipped. Microwave sugar, lemon juice and peel on HIGH until sugar dissolves. Beat eggs. Add hot mixture to eggs while beating. Microwave on HIGH until mixture is thickened, stirring several times. Cool thoroughly. Fold in whipped cream. Chill and serve over puddings or fresh fruit.

Sabayon: 4 egg yolks, 50g (2oz) sugar, 50ml (2fl oz) dry white wine, 1 × 15ml tbsp (1tbsp) framboise (raspberry brandy). Beat egg yolks and sugar until light and lemon coloured. Gradually beat in wine and brandy. Microwave on 70% power 1–3 minutes until mixture thickens into fluffy custard. (Watch carefully and stop cooking before egg yolks curdle.)

Brandied Butterscotch Sauce: 150g (6oz) dark brown sugar, pinch of salt, 100ml (4fl oz) water, 1 × 15ml tbsp (1tbsp) instant coffee, 50ml (2fl oz) brandy, 1 can 397g (14oz) sweetened condensed milk, a few drops vanilla essence. Combine sugar, salt and water and microwave on HIGH to soft-ball stage 112°C (230°F.) Dissolve coffee in brandy. Add hot syrup to milk. Blend in brandy mixture and vanilla. Stir. Makes 425ml (¾pt).

Sour Cream Sauce: 100g (4oz) brown sugar, 100ml (4fl oz) sour cream. Microwave on 50% power 1–2 minutes until sugar melts.

Maple Walnut Sauce: 325ml (12fl oz) maple syrup, 100g (4oz) coarsely chopped walnuts, toasted. Microwave syrup until it boils and stir in walnuts. Serve hot or room temperature. (Substitute corn syrup and other nuts for a nut sauce for ice cream.)

Cinnamon Syrup: 150g (6oz) brown sugar, pinch of cinnamon,

50g (2oz) butter, 100ml (4fl oz) water, 3 × 15ml tbsp (3tbsp) light corn syrup. Microwave on HIGH until mixture thickens or reaches 111°C (225°F). Serve over ice cream or fruit desserts.

Zabaglione: 4 egg yolks, 1 whole egg, 50g (2oz) sugar, pinch salt, 100ml (4fl oz) Marsala wine or sherry. Beat egg yolks, egg, sugar, and salt until thick and fluffy. Microwave Marsala on HIGH 45 seconds or until warm. Gradually beat into egg mixture. Microwave on 50% power for several minutes stirring often or until mixture is double in volume and slightly thickened. Serve warm or cold with fresh fruit or sponge fingers.

Simply Scrumptious
Cookies and Candies

Cookies — General Guidelines

Bar cookies exemplify the best of microwaving. Their taste, texture and appearance compare favourably with conventional baking and they can be ready to serve in 6–10 minutes (less time than it takes to preheat the conventional oven).

Use a square dish and shield the corners with foil, if oven permits. There is no need to grease the dish. After baking, let stand directly on the oven top 5–10 minutes to complete cooking. Cover dish with greaseproof paper.

Individual cookies must be microwaved 6–10 at a time; therefore, it is usually more efficient to bake large batches conventionally. Microwaved cookies are soft and chewy. It is difficult to make a crisp cookie. To keep dough from spreading thin and becoming too soft, the dough must be stiffer than a conventional recipe, almost crumbly. Frosting, icing sugar or crumbs add eye appeal since the cookies do not brown. To microwave, place cookies on greaseproof paper on a dish 5cm (2in) apart in a circular pattern. Microwave most cookies at 50% power. Over-baked cookies will burn in the middle.

Oatmeal Cookie Squares

Makes 16 to 24 cookies

100g (4oz) butter
100g (4oz) soft brown sugar
1 egg
Few drops vanilla essence
1 × 5ml tsp (1tsp) baking powder

115g (4½oz) quick-cooking oats
75g (3oz) flour
50g (2oz) chopped nuts
50g (2oz) raisins or chocolate, broken into small pieces

Cream butter, sugar and vanilla. Add egg and beat. Add remaining ingredients. Press mixture into 20cm (8in) square dish. Cover with clingfilm and microwave on 70% power for 4–6 minutes; uncover and cook on HIGH 1–2 minutes. Cool and cut into squares.

Oatmeal Scotchies: Instead of broken chocolate pieces, fold in butterscotch, broken into small pieces.

Children's Favourite: Instead of chocolate, immediately after cooking, lightly press miniature fruit pastilles in the top of the cookies.

Delicious Coconut Bars

Crust:
75g (3oz) butter
50g (2oz) dark brown sugar
100g (4oz) flour
50g (2oz) finely chopped pecans or walnuts

Filling:
2 eggs
225g (8oz) sugar
Few drops vanilla essence
1 × 2.5ml tsp (½tsp) baking powder
125g (5oz) coconut (toasted is better)

Combine crust ingredients and press into 22.5cm (9in) square dish. Microwave on 50% power for 3–7 minutes. Combine filling ingredients except 40g (1½oz) coconut. Pour over crust and microwave on 50% power for 5–10 minutes, until almost done in the centre. Sprinkle with remaining coconut. Microwave 1–3 minutes longer until set. Cool directly on oven top.

Variations: Make other bar cookies using the 'Delicious' crust.

Delicious Date Bars: Use Date Nut filling on page 161. Spread on baked 'Delicious' crust and microwave on HIGH 4–8 minutes until set. Sprinkle caster sugar on top.

Cheesecake Delights: 225g (8oz) cream cheese, 100g (4oz) sugar, 1 egg, 1 × 15ml tbsp (1tbsp) orange juice concentrate, 1 × 5ml tsp (1tsp) grated orange peel, 1 × 15ml tbsp (1tbsp) milk. Microwave cream cheese on 50% power about 45 seconds to soften. Add remaining ingredients. Spread on crust. Cover with clingfilm and cook on 70% power for 5–6 minutes or until set about 2.5cm (1in) from centre. Sprinkle with caster sugar.

Lemon Bars

Crust:
100g (4oz) butter
100g (4oz) flour
50g (2oz) caster sugar

Filling:
3 eggs
2 × 15ml tbsp (2tbsp) lemon juice
1 × 5ml tsp (1tsp) lemon rind
1 × 2.5ml tsp (½tsp) baking
    powder
225g (8oz) sugar
2 × 15ml tbsp (2tbsp) flour
Caster sugar

Combine crust ingredients and cut into fine crumbs with food processor or fork. Press in bottom of 22.5cm (9in) square dish. Microwave on HIGH 3–4 minutes or until surface looks dull. Mix all ingredients for filling and pour over baked crust. Cover with clingfilm and microwave on 70% power for 5–7 minutes or until set about 2.5cm (1in) from the centre. Cool covered on oven top. Sprinkle the top lightly with caster sugar and cut in bars.

Peanut Butter Bars

100g (4oz) butter
225g (8oz) dark brown sugar
100g (4oz) crunchy peanut butter
2 eggs
100g (4oz) flour

1 × 5ml tsp (1tsp) baking powder
Pinch of salt
150g (6oz) chocolate, broken in
    small pieces (optional)

Heat butter on HIGH for 30 seconds to melt. Add sugar, peanut butter and eggs. Combine flour, baking powder and salt. Add to peanut butter mixture. Stir in chocolate chips. Pour into 22.5cm (9in) square dish. Microwave on HIGH power for 5–7 minutes. Let stand on oven top to cool. When cool, cut into bars.

Chocolate Chip Pan Cookies

Makes 24 bars

100g (4oz) butter
150g (6oz) dark brown sugar
1 egg
1 × 15ml tbsp (1tbsp) milk
Few drops vanilla essence
100g (4oz) flour

1 × 2.5ml tsp (½tsp) baking
  powder
Pinch of salt
100g (4oz) chocolate pieces
50g (2oz) nuts

Cream butter and sugar. Add egg, vanilla and milk. Mix well. Combine flour, baking powder and salt. Add to creamed mixture. Blend and stir in 50g (2oz) chocolate pieces and 25g (1oz) nuts. Spread in 22.5cm (9in) square dish. Sprinkle remaining chocolate and nuts on top. Microwave on HIGH 4–7 minutes. Cool and cut into bars.

Brownies

100g (4oz) butter
6 × 15ml tbsp (6tbsp) cocoa
225g (8oz) granulated or brown
  sugar
1 egg (2 eggs for a cake-type
  brownie)

Few drops vanilla essence
75g (3oz) flour
1 × 2.5ml tsp (½tsp) baking
  powder
Pinch of salt
50g (2oz) chopped nuts

Melt butter and cocoa together. Microwave on HIGH 1–1½ minutes. Add sugar, then other ingredients. Microwave on HIGH 5½–6 minutes. Good as a bar cookie or topped with ice cream and chocolate sauce for a quick dessert.

Blond Brownies: Omit cocoa and use brown sugar instead of white. You may stir in 50g (2oz) small chocolate pieces.

Peanut Butter Frosted Brownies: Cook blond brownies. Immediately after taking out of the oven, sprinkle them with 50g (2oz) chocolate pieces and spoons of peanut butter (about 50g (2oz)). When soft, spread and swirl for marbled effect.

Butterscotch Brownies: Make Brownies recipe using brown sugar instead of white and omit the cocoa. Fold in 150g (6oz) of butterscotch, broken into small pieces.

Cheesecake Bars

Makes 30 to 40 bars

75g (3oz) butter
75g (3oz) dark brown sugar
100g (4oz) sifted flour
25g (1oz) chopped pecans or
   walnuts
50g (2oz) caster sugar

225g (8oz) cream cheese
1 egg, beaten
1 × 15ml tbsp (1tbsp) milk
1 × 15ml tbsp (1tbsp) lemon juice
Few drops vanilla essence

Cream butter and brown sugar; add flour and chopped nuts. Cream with spoon until mixture forms crumbs. Set aside 100g (4oz) of mixture for topping. Press remaining mixture into 20cm (8in) square dish. Bake on HIGH 3–3½ minutes. Combine white sugar and cream cheese. Beat until smooth. Add egg, milk, lemon juice and vanilla. Beat. Spread over baked crumbs. Sprinkle reserved crumbs over top. Cover with clingfilm and cook on 50% power for 5 minutes. Uncover and cook on HIGH 1–2 minutes. Cut into bars and store in refrigerator. Delicious!

Filled Oatmeal Bars

Base:
100g (4oz) butter
100g (4oz) brown sugar
Pinch of salt

75g (3oz) quick-cooking oats
100g (4oz) flour

Mix butter, sugar and salt. Add oats and flour. Mix to form crumbs. Reserve 100g (4oz). Press remaining mixture in a 20cm (8in) square dish. Microwave 3–7 minutes on 50% power or just until dull-looking. Spread one of the following fillings over crust. Sprinkle with reserved crumbs and microwave on HIGH 4–8 minutes.

Raspberry: 150ml (6fl oz) raspberry jam (or any jam flavour).

Mincemeat: 225ml (8fl oz) prepared mincemeat.

Date Nut: 150g (6oz) dates, 75ml (3fl oz) water, 3 × 15ml tbsp (3tbsp) sugar, 1 × 15ml tbsp (1tbsp) lemon juice, 50g (2oz) finely chopped walnuts. Combine ingredients, except walnuts, and microwave on HIGH 3–5 minutes, or until thick and smooth, stirring several times. Add nuts.

Chocolate: 225ml (8fl oz) sweetened condensed milk, 100g (4oz) chocolate pieces, 50g (2oz) nuts, optional. Cook milk on HIGH 1 minute. Stir in chocolate pieces and nuts. Stir to melt chocolate. Microwave an additional 30 seconds if needed.

Butterscotch: Same as for chocolate, but use butterscotch pieces.

Caramel: 1 × 397g (14oz) can condensed milk, 2 × 15ml tbsp (2tbsp) milk, 50g (2oz) nuts, optional. Cook condensed milk in a Pyrex measure on 40% power for 12–15 minutes, stirring occasionally, until milk is caramel coloured and thick. Fold in 2 × 15ml tbsp (2tbsp) milk and nuts.

Lemon Cheese: 225g (8oz) cream cheese, 75g (3oz) sugar, 1 egg, 1 × 15ml tbsp (1tbsp) lemon juice, 1 × 5ml tsp (1tsp) grated lemon peel, 2 × 15ml tbsp (2tbsp) milk. Soften cream cheese by microwaving on HIGH about 45 seconds. Add remaining ingredients.

Prune: 150g (6oz) pitted prunes, 75ml (3fl oz) water, 100g (4oz) brown sugar, 1 × 15ml tbsp (1tbsp) lemon juice, pinch of salt, 25g (1oz) chopped walnuts (optional). Combine and microwave on HIGH 3–5 minutes, stirring several times. Purée in blender. You may want to add 1 × 2.5ml tsp (½tsp) ground cinnamon to the base mixture.

Date Balls

150g (6oz) butter
225g (8oz) chopped, pitted dates
150g (6oz) sugar
50g (2oz) chopped nuts or 40g
    (1½oz) desiccated coconut

50g (2oz) Rice Krispies
Caster or icing sugar, optional

Combine butter, sugar and dates. Microwave on HIGH 3½–6 minutes or until thickened. Cool slightly. Add nuts or coconut and Rice Krispies. Roll into balls about 2.5cm (1in) in diameter. Roll in sugar if preferred.

♥ Use flavoured sugars to garnish cookies. To flavour sugar, drop a vanilla pod, slightly dried lemon peel or orange peel into a small container of sugar. Keep closed several days or longer.

Crème de Menthe Squares

Makes 40 to 45 pieces

Crust:
75g (3oz) butter
25g (1oz) cocoa
150g (6oz) digestive biscuit crumbs
50g (2oz) caster sugar
1 egg
Few drops vanilla essence

Filling:
75g (3oz) butter
50ml (2fl oz) crème de menthe
  (green)
450g (1lb) icing sugar

Topping:
50g (2oz) butter
150g (6oz) chocolate pieces

Melt butter for crust by microwaving on HIGH. Add cocoa, then other ingredients. Press into 20cm (8in) square dish and micro-wave 1½–3½ minutes on 50% power.

Melt butter for filling. Add crème de menthe and sugar. Spread over chocolate layer and chill.

Make topping by melting together butter and chocolate chips on 70% power for 2–3 minutes. Stir and pour over green layer. Chill and cut in small squares. Very rich!

Crème d'Almonde Squares: Substitute Crème d'Almonde (red) or other almond liqueur for crème de menthe. If liqueur is clear in colour, a few drops of red food colouring may be added to make a pink filling. You may garnish with a slice of almond on top of the chocolate.

Sherry Cream Dreams: Substitute 1 × 15ml tbsp (1tbsp) sherry, 1 × 15ml tbsp (1tbsp) milk, and 50g (2oz) chopped walnuts for the crème de menthe.

♨ To soften brown sugar, add a few drops of water or a slice of apple to the box and microwave on HIGH 15 seconds.

♨ When baking cookies conventionally, test a few in the microwave. You'll soon learn which ones are suitable for microwaving.

♨ Pink almond and green mint fillings are especially pretty at Christmas.

Candies

General Guidelines

Both old-fashioned cooked candies and short-cut candies micro-wave easily. Candy will not scorch since there is no direct heat. It needs stirring only a couple of times during cooking to equalise heat. Usually 70% power is best to keep candy from boiling over. Sugar becomes very hot when boiled. Use a container that can withstand high temperatures and is 2 to 3 times the volume of the candy ingredients. A 2 litre (3½pt) ovenproof measuring jug is ideal since it is deep and has a handle.

A conventional mercury thermometer cannot be used in the microwave oven when the oven is operating; it will be damaged and will not register accurately. Check the syrup temperature with the thermometer as soon as the oven door is opened to get an accurate reading. You may prefer the cold water tests to determine if the candy is cooked. COLD WATER TESTS: Fill a cup with cold water; drop about 1 × 2.5ml tsp (½tsp) of boiling candy syrup into the cold water. Pick up the ball to judge its consistency and how much it is cooked.

Candy	Test in Cold Water	Degrees on Candy Thermometer
Fudge Fondant	Soft ball (can be picked up but flattens)	114°C–115°C (238°F–240°F)
Caramels	Firm ball (holds shape unless pressed)	115.5°C–121°C (242°F–250°F)
Fancies Caramel Popcorn	Hard ball (holds shape though pliable)	121°C–130°C (250°F–268°F)
Butterscotch Toffee	Soft crack (separates into hard threads but not brittle)	131°C–145°C (270°F–290°F)
Brittles	Hard crack (separates into hard and brittle threads)	150°C–155°C (300°F–310°F)

Simply Scrumptious Butterscotch Fudge

This is a truly creamy, delicious fudge An old-fashioned fudge made from an up-to-date recipe. Be sure to try each variation. By altering the ingredients you can make several scrumptious flavours.

Makes 48 pieces

50g (2oz) butter	150ml (6fl oz) sour cream
225g (8oz) brown sugar	Few drops vanilla essence
225g (8oz) granulated or caster sugar	50g (2oz) chopped walnuts

Microwave butter in a deep bowl on HIGH about 1 minute or until melted. Add brown sugar and heat to boiling by microwave on 50%–70% power for 3 to 4 minutes. Add remaining sugar and sour cream. Microwave on 50%–70% power for 15–20 minutes to soft ball stage, 114°C (238°F). Without stirring, cool at room temperature to lukewarm. Beat with the electric mixer until mixture holds its shape and loses its gloss. Quickly add vanilla and nuts. Spread immediately in a buttered 20cm (8in) square dish. Cool and cut into squares. Garnish with additional nuts if desired.

Simply Scrumptious Vanilla Fudge: Make Butterscotch Fudge using 450g (1lb) granulated sugar and no brown sugar.

Simply Scrumptious Chocolate Fudge: Make Butterscotch Fudge following the recipe exactly, but adding 3 to 4 squares bitter plain chocolate with the sour cream.

♥ This fudge is delicious to use as centres for dipped chocolates. Just form the fudge into balls or desired shapes, chill thoroughly and dip in chocolate.

Uncooked Fudge

450g (1lb) icing sugar, sifted
100g (4oz) butter
25g (1oz) cocoa

50ml (2fl oz) milk
Few drops vanilla essence

Microwave butter, cocoa and sugar on HIGH 2 minutes, stirring a time or two as butter melts. Add milk and vanilla. Microwave on HIGH 1 minute longer. Pour into a 20cm (8in) square dish and freeze ½ hour.

Fast Scotch Fudge

350g (12oz) butterscotch pieces
1 × 397g (14oz) can condensed milk

1 × 350g (12oz) can smooth peanut butter

Microwave butterscotch pieces on HIGH 2–3 minutes until melted. Stir in other ingredients and cook on HIGH 1–2 minutes longer until bubbly. Pour in buttered 20cm (8in) square dish. Refrigerate until set. Cut in squares.

Fast Rum Fudge

500g (18oz) plain chocolate pieces
1 × 397g (14oz) can condensed milk

Pinch of salt
225g (8oz) chopped walnuts
2 × 15ml tbsp (2tbsp) dark rum

Melt chocolate chips in mixing bowl. Microwave 2–3 minutes on 70% power or until melted, stirring several times. Add milk and salt, beat until smooth. Stir in rum and nuts. Spread evenly in a 20cm (8in) dish and refrigerate until hardened.

🦃 'Uncooked' candies have a better flavour if microwaved for a minute or two.

🦃 Fast Fudge has a texture of caramels. For a texture change, beat the mixture on high speed with an electric mixer after all ingredients have been added, except nuts and fruits, for 3–5 minutes. Chill 5 minutes and beat again to achieve a lighter, creamier texture.

Fast Chocolate Fudge

Makes 36 pieces

275–350g (10–12oz) plain
chocolate pieces
1 × 397g (14oz) can condensed
milk

50g (2oz) butter
100g (4oz) chopped pecans or
walnuts

Microwave chocolate, milk and butter on 50%–70% power until chocolate melts, 3–5 minutes, stirring several times. Add nuts and pour into a well buttered 20cm (8in) square baking dish. Refrigerate until set.

Peppermint Fudge Omit nuts and add a few drops of peppermint oil.

Fast Vanilla Fudge

350g (12oz) white chocolate
1 × 397g (14oz) can condensed
milk

50g (2oz) butter

Microwave chocolate, milk and butter on 50% power until chocolate melts, 3–5 minutes, stirring several times. Pour into well buttered 20cm (8in) square dish. Chill until firm and cut in 2.5cm (1in) squares. Store in covered containers.

Variations: After cooking, stir in one of the following additions:

150g (6oz) almonds and a few drops almond essence
150g (6oz) chopped dates and 100g (4oz) chopped walnuts
150g (6oz) chopped candied fruit

Chocolate Leaves: Wash a rose leaf. Melt chocolate pieces. Pull a single leaf upside down over surface of melted chocolate. Remove extra chocolate by shaking leaf slightly and tapping against side of the bowl. Place leaf, chocolate side up on baking sheet to harden. (Make a curved leaf by letting it dry over curved surface such as cardboard tube.) Then peel off leaf. Veins of the real leaf will be imprinted in the chocolate. An elegant dessert garnish. Butterscotch pieces may be used instead of chocolate.

Bark Candy

Bark Candy is a good way to use bits of leftover dipping chocolate. Pour melted chocolate coating or real chocolate over toasted nuts. Cool and break into serving-sized pieces.

Almond Bark: Makes 675g (1½lb). 150g (6oz) blanched almonds, 450g (1lb) white chocolate. Toast almonds by spreading them in a single layer in a pie plate and microwaving on HIGH 4–7 minutes until toasted. Let stand about 2 minutes. Melt chocolate by microwaving on 50% power until softened, 2–3 minutes. Stir in almonds and spread on baking sheet and refrigerate. Break into pieces.

Variations: Other Bark combinations may be made by using other flavour coatings such as chocolate, butterscotch or caramel; and other nuts such as walnuts, peanuts, pecans, coconuts or dates, raisins or mixed nuts, or candied fruit bits.

Marbled Bark Candy: Makes 900g (2lb). 900g (2lb) white chocolate, 25g (1oz) butter, 3 or 4 drops oil flavouring (peppermint, orange, spearmint, etc). Colouring, use paste or powdered colouring or tinted chocolate. Place 450g (1lb) chocolate and 15g (½oz) butter in a dish to melt. Place the remaining chocolate and butter, flavouring and colouring in another dish to melt. Melt the coloured, flavoured mixture by microwaving on 50% power for 2–3 minutes. Stir to combine. When smooth, spread thinly on greaseproof paper. Immediately microwave the white chocolate on 50% power for 2–3 minutes to melt. Stir until smooth; pour over the tinted chocolate in a swirled pattern. With a knife or spatula, cut through both colours to create a marbled effect. Let candy harden and break in pieces.

🔥 Try using milk chocolate or dark chocolate marbled with another colour; for example, dark chocolate and green mint flavoured white chocolate.

🔥 Microwave candy thermometers are available. They register up to 160°C (320°F) and can be used in the oven during microwaving.

Toffee

Makes 450g (1lb)

225g (8oz) butter
275g (10oz) sugar
1 × 15ml tbsp (1tbsp) golden
  syrup
2 × 15ml tbsp (2tbsp) water

Few drops vanilla essence
75g (3oz) chocolate, broken into
  fine pieces
50g (2oz) finely chopped pecans or
  walnuts

Combine butter, sugar, syrup and water in a deep bowl and microwave on 70% power 15–20 minutes or to hard crack stage 150°C (300°F). Stir in vanilla. Pour into buttered 32.5 × 22.5cm (13 × 9in) pan. Sprinkle with chocolate pieces. After 2 minutes spread them over the toffee. Sprinkle with nuts and lightly press into chocolate. Chill. Break into pieces.

Walnut Fancies

Makes about 30 pieces

450g (1lb) granulated sugar
100ml (4fl oz) cold water
1 × 5ml tsp (1tsp) vinegar

1 egg white
Few drops vanilla essence
25g (1oz) chopped walnuts

Combine sugar, water and vinegar in a deep bowl. Microwave covered on 70% power for 12–15 minutes or until candy reaches 11.5°C (242°F) (firm ball). Meanwhile, beat egg white until stiff peaks form. Pour syrup in a thin stream into the egg white, while beating constantly with electric mixer. Add vanilla; beat until stiff. Fold in nuts. Drop by teaspoonfuls onto greaseproof paper; cool.

Variations may be made by making the following substitutions.

Maple Nut Fancies: Use half white sugar and half brown sugar. Substitute maple flavouring for vanilla and chopped pecans for walnuts.

Harlequin Fancies: Use 50g (2oz) chopped walnuts and 25g (1oz) chopped candied cherries. Add food colourings as desired to make pastel colours.

Almond Chocolate Cream Centres
Simply Scrumptious!

Makes 4–5 dozen

225ml (8fl oz) whipping cream
275g (10oz) plain chocolate, finely
  chopped
40g (1½oz) butter
25g (1oz) coarsely chopped toasted
  almonds

50ml (2fl oz) amaretto
Few drops almond essence
450–675g (1–1½lb) plain
  chocolate

Microwave cream on HIGH 1–2 minutes to simmering. Add chocolate and butter. Whisk until smooth. Cool to lukewarm. Stir in almonds, amaretto and essence. Cover and refrigerate until firm, 4 hours or overnight. Make 2.5cm (1in) balls. Freeze uncovered until hard. Dip in chocolate.

Brazil Nut Creams: Substitute toasted brazil nuts for almonds, and white chocolate for plain chocolate. Before coating sets, lightly sift cocoa over dipped truffles.

Kirsch Chocolate Creams: Substitute 3 × 15ml tbsp (3tbsp) kirsch for amaretto and essence.

Caramel Centres: Microwave the contents of 1 × 397g (14oz) can condensed milk in a deep bowl at 40% power about 12–15 minutes until it caramelises. Stir several times during cooking. Stir in 4 × 15ml tbsp (4tbsp) milk. Cool and shape into balls. (Add 50g (2oz) nuts if desired.) Refrigerate several hours and dip in chocolate.

🔆 Make candy patties instead of balls and dip in chocolate.

Simply Scrumptious Chocolates
Truffles, bonbons and other delights

When cooking with chocolate, the biggest advantage of the microwave oven is the absence of direct heat. If chocolate is overcooked, it will become bitter and grainy. Microwave on 70% power to heat chocolate gently. Breaking chocolate into smaller pieces promotes even and faster melting. (Food processors are ideal.)

Never cover when melting chocolate. Steam will condense on

the bottom of the lid; water in chocolate will cause it to thicken and loose its shine. Never add water, milk or other liquids directly to chocolate. Use oil flavourings, never alcohol or water base. White chocolate may be coloured by using a paste or powdered colouring, not liquid food colouring.

When microwaving chocolate, the chocolate will retain its shape, but the appearance will change from dull to shiny. The chocolate will be softened, and stirring will mix the melted chocolate so that it is liquid and smooth. When it will not melt properly, it is probably old or has absorbed moisture. Stir about 1 × 15ml tbsp (1tbsp) coconut or vegetable oil in to assist melting.

Store chocolate tightly wrapped since it readily absorbs odours. Never store in the freezer or refrigerator, it may become damp and not melt. Store in a plastic bag in a cool dry place.

The quality of chocolate varies with manufacturers. Select a good quality. Poor-quality chocolate will make waxy, poor-quality candy. The difference between real chocolate and chocolate-flavoured coatings is the oil base used in the product. Real chocolate is better quality, more expensive and requires more skill. Beginners may choose to use a coating, then move to real chocolate since chocolate coating is easier to work with.

🐟 The secret of successful candy making lies in dissolving the sugar slowly. Microwave at a reduced power level of 70% or lower for best results.

Swiss Chocolate Gnache

350ml (12fl oz) whipping cream   225g (8oz) plain chocolate, finely chopped

Microwave cream on HIGH 1–2 minutes to simmering. Add chocolate and whip till thick. Consistency should be that of whipped cream. Cool, refrigerate 4 hours or overnight until firm. Make 2.5cm (1in) balls. Freeze centres, uncovered, 4 hours. Dip in chocolate.

These centres are soft to handle. That's why freezing is needed before dipping. However, the results are worth the effort. The finished candies have a creamy delicious centre.

Grand Marnier Gnache: Add 3 × 15ml tbsp (3tbsp) Grand Marnier to cooled Gnache. Ater dipping, garnish top of bonbons with small pieces of candied orange peel if desired.

Mocha Gnache: Add 3 × 15ml tbsp (3tbsp) instant coffee and finely chopped nuts (optional) to cooled Gnache.

Cordial Creams: Add 3 × 15ml tbsp (3tbsp) whisky or any preferred liqueur to cooled Ganache. Cherry liqueur is delicious! Try crème de menthe, too.

Chocolate Coffee Truffles
A very rich creamy centre

Makes 4–5 dozen

225g (8oz) plain chocolate	50ml (2fl oz) coffee liqueur
3 egg yolks	100g (4oz) butter

Melt chocolate on 50% power for 3–4 minutes. Stir until smooth. Beat in egg yolks one at a time. Blend in liqueur. Microwave on 70% power for 1 minute. Add softened butter a little at a time while beating. Continue beating 4–5 minutes. Freeze several hours. Form into 2.5cm (1in) balls. Return to freezer several hours to chill thoroughly. Dip in chocolate.

Crunchy Delights
Simply Scrumptious peanut butter centres

225g (8oz) crushed digestive biscuits	225g (8oz) peanut butter
	225g (8oz) icing sugar
75g (3oz) coconut	Few drops vanilla essence
100g (4oz) chopped pecans or walnuts	225g (8oz) melted butter

Mix all ingredients. Roll into 2.5cm (1in) balls. Dip in melting chocolate.

Delicious Bonbons

Coconut Bonbons: In a deep bowl, microwave 100ml (4fl oz) golden syrup on HIGH for 1–2 minutes or to gentle boil. Add coconut to give a stiff mixture. Mix thoroughly. Cool. Roll mixture into 2.5cm (1in) balls. Chill and dip in chocolate.

Easy Home-made Fondant: Gradually add 900g (2lb) caster sugar to 150ml (6fl oz) condensed milk. Add 1 × 1.25ml tsp (¼tsp) salt and a few drops vanilla essence. Sprinkle icing sugar on a board and knead fondant until smooth and creamy. Wrap in clingfilm and place in refrigerator for 24 hours. Can be flavoured and used as cream centres.

Chocolate Covered Cherries: Wrap Easy Home-made Fondant around a maraschino cherry and dip in chocolate.

Peanut Cream Centres: 50g (2oz) caster sugar, 100ml (4fl oz) condensed milk, 225g (8oz) creamy peanut butter, 150g (6oz) chocolate pieces, 7 × 15ml tbsp (7tbsp) chocolate vermicelli. Combine sugar, milk and peanut butter in a medium mixing bowl. Stir until well blended. Stir in chocolate and chill until firm. Shape into small balls and roll each in chocolate vermicelli. Refrigerate until firm. Makes 6 dozen.

Butterscotch Creams: 100g (4oz) butterscotch pieces, 225g (8oz) cream cheese, 350g (12oz) caster sugar. Microwave butterscotch on 70% power 2–3 minutes. Add cream cheese, then sugar. Spread in buttered dish and chill. Remove from refrigerator and form into 2.5cm (1in) balls. Freeze, dip in melted chocolate and chopped nuts.

Crunchy Peanut Butter Centre: 450g (1lb) crunchy peanut butter, 100g (4oz) margarine, 450g (1lb) icing sugar, 225g (8oz) Rice Krispies. Combine all ingredients except cereal and form into 2.5cm (1in) balls. Add cereal. Chill and dip in chocolate.

Chocolate Covered Pretzels: Melt chocolate to dipping consistency. Drop a few pretzels in and lift out with fork. Hold to let drain slightly. Place on baking sheet to harden.

Chocolate Covered Nuts: Dip almonds, pecans or other nuts in chocolate. Try white chocolate for a change.

Penoche
Old-fashioned candy recipe

675g (1½lb) sugar
50ml (2fl oz) golden syrup

150ml (6fl oz) milk
225g (8oz) nuts, pecans or peanuts

Caramelise 225g (8oz) sugar by mixing it with 1 × 15ml tbsp (1tbsp) water and microwaving on HIGH about 2–2½ minutes until it liquefies and is a caramel colour. Mix remaining sugar with the other ingredients and microwave on HIGH until it boils. Add caramelised sugar and microwave on 70% power 15–20 minutes to soft-ball stage. (Reduce power level to 50% if necessary to keep syrup from boiling over.) Cool slightly and pour into mixer bowl. Beat until candy holds shape. Drop by tablespoonful on a sheet of greaseproof paper.

Peanut Brittle

Makes 450g (1lb)

150g (6oz) raw peanuts
225g (8oz) white sugar
100ml (4fl oz) golden syrup
Pinch of salt

Few drops vanilla essence
15g (½oz) butter
2 × 5ml tsp (2tsp) bicarbonate of soda

Stir peanuts, sugar, syrup and salt together in deep bowl. Cook on HIGH 4 minutes. Stir candy so all sugar is mixed and continue cooking on HIGH 3 more minutes. Add butter and vanilla to syrup, blending well. Cook on HIGH 1–3 minutes. Add bicarbonate of soda and stir until light and foamy. Pour immediately onto lightly buttered surface, spreading it out. Cool and break into pieces. Store in airtight container. If roasted salted peanuts are used, omit salt and add peanuts after first 4 minutes of cooking.

🖙 For interesting Brittle variations, try almonds, pecans, peanuts, cashews, walnuts, coconuts or combinations in either of the Brittle recipes. Also try using brown sugar instead of white.

Pecan Butter Brittle

225g (8oz) pecan halves
225g (8oz) sugar
100ml (4fl oz) golden syrup

50g (2oz) butter
2 × 5ml tsp (2tsp) bicarbonate of
 soda

Microwave sugar, syrup and butter 3 minutes on HIGH. Stir in nuts. Mix well and microwave on HIGH 7–12 minutes, checking nuts several times to make sure they don't burn. Add bicarbonate of soda, quickly stir and pour onto greased surface. Cool and break into pieces. Store in airtight container.

Caramel Popcorn Balls

225g (8oz) light brown sugar
50g (2oz) butter
100ml (4fl oz) golden syrup
½ of a 397g (14oz) can sweetened
 condensed milk

Few drops vanilla essence
3.5 litres (6½pt) popped corn

Combine sugar, butter and syrup in a deep bowl. Cook on HIGH 2–3 minutes until butter melts. Add milk and microwave on 70% power until soft-ball stage is reached (114°C (238°F) for 5–7 minutes). Stir in vanilla and pour over popped corn. Mix with buttered hands and roll into balls. Try adding raisins or peanuts with the popped corn.

Butterscotch Nut Squares

150g (6oz) butterscotch pieces
150g (6oz) chocolate pieces
1 × 397g (14oz) can condensed
 milk

100g (4oz) pecans, chopped
Few drops vanilla essence
100g (4oz) pecan halves

Combine butterscotch, chocolate and condensed milk in a 2 litre (3½pt) glass casserole. Microwave on 70% power for 4–6 minutes, stirring occasionally until butterscotch and chocolate melt and candy begins to thicken. Add chopped nuts and vanilla and stir to blend. Pour candy into a buttered 20cm (8in) square dish. Top with pecan halves. Chill in refrigerator until firm enough to slice.

Lollipops

10 lollipop sticks
150g (6oz) sugar
100ml (4fl oz) golden syrup
50g (2oz) butter

1 × 5ml tsp (1tsp) flavouring
(peppermint, orange, vanilla,
cinnamon, etc)
Food colouring
Miniature sweets for decoration

Arrange sticks on parchment paper, spacing at least 10cm (4in) apart. Combine sugar, golden syrup and butter in 2 litre (3½pt) measuring jug or bowl and cook on HIGH 2 minutes. Stir in flavouring and food colouring. Continue cooking on HIGH until candy thermometer registers 131°C (270°F) or soft-crack stage, about 5–7 minutes.

Drop syrup by tablespoons over one end of each stick. Press sweets gently into place. Let cool completely. Wrap each in clingfilm. Store in airtight container.

Toffee Apples: Use cinnamon flavouring and red colouring. Insert sticks into about 6 apples and dip the apples one at a time into the cooked syrup. Swirl to coat; then stand on greaseproof paper to cool.

Candied Citrus Peel

Makes 400ml (16fl oz)
225g (8oz) peel (orange,
  grapefruit, lime, etc)
225g (8oz) sugar

Pinch of salt
100ml (4fl oz) water

Cut the peel into narrow strips and cover with water. Microwave on HIGH for 10 minutes and drain. Cover with fresh water and microwave on HIGH 10 additional minutes. Add drained peel to an ovenproof bowl with sugar and 100ml (4fl oz) water. Microwave on HIGH for 12 to 16 minutes, stirring several times. Cool and roll each piece in sugar.

Variation: Add one packet of fruit-flavoured jelly crystals to sugar and toss peel in this mixture.

Peanut Butter Squares

50g (2oz) digestive biscuit crumbs
225g (8oz) chunky peanut butter
550g (1¼lb) caster sugar

225g (8oz) melted butter
225g (8oz) milk chocolate, broken
  into pieces

Mix crumbs, sugar, butter and peanut butter. Spread in a 22.5cm × 32.5cm (9 × 13in) dish. Shield ends of dish with foil, if oven permits. Microwave on HIGH 2 minutes to set. Melt chocolate by microwaving on 50% power for 3–4 minutes. Spread on mixture while warm. Chill and cut in squares.

Simply Scrumptious White Fudge

Makes about 60 pieces

275g (10oz) sugar
100g (4oz) butter
150ml (6fl oz) cream
Pinch of salt

225g (8oz) white chocolate, finely
  chopped
100g (4oz) marshmallows cut into
  pieces
1 × 2.5ml tsp (½tsp) vanilla

Microwave sugar, butter, cream and salt on 50%–70% power about 20–30 minutes or to 114°C (238°F), soft-ball stage. Add chocolate, marshmallow and vanilla. Blend well and pack into a 22.5cm (9in) square tin and cut into squares when partially cool.

Before completely cooled, White Fudge has a pliable texture like dough. It can easily be rolled into balls or other desired shapes for dipping in chocolate.

🖐 Make a candy assortment from one recipe using various flavourings and fruits: chopped candied or dried fruits, nuts of any kinds, raisins, dates or coconut.

Maple nut: Add several drops of maple flavouring and finely chopped pecans or walnuts.

Coffee: Dissolve instant coffee in a few drops of water. Microwave a few seconds if needed.

🖐 Divide fudge in half. Flavour and colour half as desired. Roll out each half separately. Lay one on top of the other and roll up like a Catherine wheel. Chill thoroughly and slice.

Simply Scrumptious
Preserves, Freezing Vegetables, Drying Flowers and Herbs

Jams, Jellies and Relishes

Jams, jellies and relishes cooked in the microwave have a fresh flavour that is not achieved by conventional methods of cooking or processing, therefore you may prefer to microwave small amounts rather than prepare large batches that would require water-bath processing needed for long storage.

Cook in a deep dish. Sterilise jars by filling them half-full of water and microwaving on HIGH until the water boils vigorously. Metal jar lids must be treated conventionally following the manufacturer's directions.

The test for setting for microwaved jams and jellies is the same 'sheet' test as for conventional jams, even when using commercial fruit pectin. Dip a large metal spoon in the boiling jam, holding it up out of the steam and turning the spoon so the syrup runs off the edge. When the drops run together and drop off the spoon in a sheet, the setting point has been reached.

To seal jelly, pour boiling hot jelly into sterilised hot jars leaving 3mm (⅛in) head space. Screw prepared metal lid on firmly and allow jelly to set upright, undisturbed until cool. A vacuum seal will form as the jelly cools.

For jams, conserves or marmalades, remove the product from the microwave and stir gently for 5 minutes. This will allow the syrup to thicken slightly and help keep the fruit dispersed throughout. Skim the foam that appears on the surface. Pour inot hot glass containers to within 1.3cm (½in) of top. (This procedure is exactly the same in conventional preserving.) Seal immediately.

For long term storage, jams, preserves, marmalades and conserves should be processed in a boiling water-bath (conventional method). Jelly and jam recipes offered by Simply Scrumptious require 5 minutes processing time.

Simply Scrumptious Strawberry Jam
Wonderful fresh strawberry flavour

Makes 1kg (2lb)
450g (1lb) fresh strawberries
450g (1lb) sugar
2 × 15ml tbsp (2tbsp) lemon juice

Wash and stem strawberries, drain in colander and place in a 2.8 litre (5pt) ovenproof bowl. Stir in lemon juice. Microwave on HIGH for 5 minutes, stirring several times. Add sugar and stir till dissolved. Microwave on HIGH for about 15 minutes or until setting point is reached (105°C 221°F). Stir every 5 minutes. Leave to cool slightly, stir and pour into sterilised jars. Cover and label in the usual way.

Fresh Peach Jam

Makes 1.1–1.4 litre (2–2½pt)

450ml (16fl oz) coarse peach purée
(peel fresh peaches and chop in
blender to desired consistency)

2 × 15ml tbsp (2tbsp) lemon juice
550g (1¼lb) sugar

Measure purée into a 2.8 litre (5pt) glass bowl. Stir in lemon juice. Microwave on HIGH for 2 minutes and 15 seconds. Add sugar and microwave on HIGH 3–4 minutes, stirring several times. Test for setting. Stir 5 minutes. Pour into sterilised jars and seal.

Spiced Peach Jam: To Fresh Peach Jam add 1 × 2.5ml tsp (½tsp) cinnamon, pinch of cloves, good pinch of mixed spice. Good served as a jam on toast, to flavour cream cheese or served with ham or chicken.

Banana Jam
Great with peanut butter sandwiches or ice cream

Makes 550ml (1pt)

690ml (1¼pt) sliced, ripe bananas
350g (12oz) sugar
50ml (2fl oz) orange juice

3 × 15ml tbsp (3tbsp) lemon juice
1 small cinnamon stick
2 whole cloves

Combine all ingredients in a deep bowl. Microwave on HIGH until sugar dissolves, 5–10 minutes, stirring several times. Continue cooking on HIGH until thickened, about 8–12 minutes. Pour into jars and let stand until set. Refrigerate.

Pineapple Jam

Makes about 1.1 litre (2pt)

1 × 566g (20oz) can unsweetened,
crushed pineapple or 1 large
finely chopped fresh pineapple
800g (1¾lb) sugar

½ lemon, thinly sliced
75ml (3fl oz) fruit pectin
100g (4oz) chopped walnuts
(optional)

Combine ingredients except nuts and microwave on HIGH for 12–15 minutes or until pineapple is soft. Add walnuts and stir until thickened. Pour into sterilised jars, and seal.

Berry Jam

Blackberry, raspberry, gooseberry, loganberry.

Makes 1.5kg (3lb)

675g (1½lb) fresh berries, washed and drained

1 × 15ml tbsp (1tbsp) lemon juice
675g (1½lb) sugar

Wash berries in a deep bowl. Stir in lemon juice. Microwave on HIGH 10–15 minutes, stirring several times or until mixture comes to a full boil. Stir in sugar. Microwave on HIGH 5–7 minutes or until mixture returns to a full boil and reaches setting point. Pour into sterilised jars and seal.

🔥 For seedless jam, crushed berries may be microwaved until soft and pressed through a sieve; then add lemon juice and proceed as above.

Jiffy Spiced Fruit
Good fresh flavour

3 large peaches, pears, apricots or nectarines, peeled and halved
100ml (4fl oz) cider vinegar
50g (2oz) sugar

Pinch of ginger
1 × 7.5cm (3in) cinnamon stick
6 whole cloves

Combine vinegar, sugar, and spices in a deep bowl. Cover with clingfilm and microwave on HIGH for 4 minutes or until sugar dissolves, stirring several times. Add fruit and stir to coat with syrup. Re-cover and cook on HIGH 6 minutes or until fruit is tender. Cool and refrigerate overnight to blend flavours. Serve chilled as a meat accompaniment or on the relish tray. Will keep in the refrigerator up to a month. Remove spices after second week.

🔥 CHESTNUTS: Slash crosswise through skin on flat end of chestnut shell. On a glass pie plate, arrange 20–25 chestnuts. Microwave on HIGH 3–4 minutes, stirring every minute until nuts are soft when squeezed. Rest 5 minutes. Peel and eat warm.

Plum Conserve

Makes 550ml (1pt)

450g (1lb) plums, pitted and chopped
1 orange, seeded and chopped
2 × 15ml tbsp (2tbsp) thinly sliced orange peel (optional)

100g (4oz) sugar or to taste
100g (4oz) chopped walnuts or pecans (optional)

Microwave plums, sugar, oranges and orange rind, covered tightly with clingfilm on HIGH 8 minutes, stirring once. Stir in nuts, re-cover and microwave on HIGH 2 minutes longer or until peel is transparent. Let stand covered 5 minutes. Chill.

Onion Pepper Relish

Makes about 225g (8oz)

1 small red pepper
1 small green pepper
2 onions, chopped
100ml (4fl oz) vinegar

50g (2oz) sugar
1 × 2.5ml tsp (½tsp) salt
1 bay leaf

Wash, seed and dice peppers. Stir all ingredients together in a deep bowl. Cover and microwave on HIGH for 5 minutes. Stir, reduce power to 70% and cook covered for 10 minutes longer. Let stand, covered 5 minutes. Remove bay leaf, stir and store in the refrigerator.

Pint o' Pickles

Makes 550ml (1pt)

100ml (4fl oz) cider vinegar
50g (2oz) sugar
1 × 2.5ml tsp (½tsp) salt
1 × 5ml tsp (1tsp) mixed pickling spice

350g (12oz) sliced cucumbers
1 small onion, thinly sliced

Microwave vinegar, sugar and spices on HIGH 4 minutes, stirring once. Add cucumbers and onion. Stir to coat. Cover with clingfilm and microwave on HIGH 3 minutes. Stir, re-cover, and cook on HIGH 1 minute longer. Let stand, covered, for 10 minutes. Spoon into jar, cover and chill before serving.

Apple Jelly

Makes 1–1.1 litre (1³/₄–2pt)
450ml (16fl oz) apple juice
550g (1¼lb) sugar

2 × 15ml tbsp (2tbsp) lemon juice

Combine apple juice and sugar in a deep bowl. Microwave on HIGH 5–7 minutes or until mixture boils. Add lemon juice. Microwave on HIGH 5–10 minutes or to 'sheet' test. Skim and pour into sterilised jars and seal. Reduce power level during cooking if needed to prevent boiling over.

Green Pepper Jelly

Makes 1 litre (1³/₄pt)
2 medium green peppers
150ml (6fl oz) cider vinegar
800g (1³/₄lb) sugar
75ml (3fl oz) fruit pectin
Green food colouring

2 × 15ml tbsp (2tbsp) fresh hot pepper or 1–2 × 15ml tbsp (1–2tbsp) crushed dried pepper

Remove seeds from pepper. Grind peppers in blender. Mix with vinegar, sugar and hot pepper. Microwave on HIGH 5–10 minutes or to gentle boil. Add liquid pectin and continue microwaving on HIGH until mixture comes to a full boil again; cook for 1 minute.

Pour through strainer into bowl, spoon off foam and add a few drops of green food colouring. Pour into sterilised jars and seal. Serve on top of cream cheese with crackers or with meats.

Cranberry-Orange Relish

Serves 8 to 10
450g (1lb) fresh cranberries
2 medium oranges
450g (1lb) sugar

100g (4oz) chopped nuts (optional)

Quarter oranges, remove seeds and chop in blender. Clean cranberries. Place all ingredients in a deep dish and microwave on HIGH 15–20 minutes or until cranberries are soft. Stir several times. Store in refrigerator.

Freezing Vegetables

The microwave oven is a good partner to your vegetable plot. It is a real convenience when preparing small amounts of food for the freezer. You may prefer to use the traditional boiling water method when freezing large quantities. However, remember that only 1.1–1.75 litre (2–3pt) of vegetables should be blanched at one time.

Vegetables require scalding (blanching) to stop the action of natural enzymes that cause changes in the food. Blanching prolongs the storage life of the food. Vegetables may be blanched in the microwave without the large amounts of boiling water required conventionally; therefore, they retain water soluble vitamins, flavour and texture that are lost in conventional methods. Follow suggested blanching times. Both over-blanching and under-blanching reduce quality.

General Procedure: Prepare vegetable, wash, peel, slice or cube. Blanch only 450g (1lb) at a time. Place vegetables and water in a dish and cover. Do not add salt. Mirowave the suggested time, stirring halfway through blanching. Place vegetables in ice-cold water to cool them quickly and immediately stop the cooking process. Let them stay in the cold water a few minutes, or until cooled. Drain thoroughly. Package, label, and quick freeze. Be sure to use a moisture-vapour-proof packaging material.

BLANCHING CHART

Vegetable	Quantity	Amount Water	Minutes on HIGH
Asparagus	450g (1lb)	50ml (2fl oz)	2½–4
Beans	450g (1lb)	100ml (4fl oz)	3½–5½
Broccoli	450g (1lb)	100ml (4fl oz)	3–5
Carrots, sliced	450g (1lb)	50ml (2fl oz)	3½–5½
Cauliflower (florets)	450g (1lb)	none	3–5
Corn-on-the-cob	4 ears	none	3½–4½
Corn, whole kernel	4 ears, cut off	50ml (2fl oz)	3½–5
Peas, green	450g (1lb)	none	3½–5
Spinach	450g (1lb)	50ml (2fl oz)	2–3½

For vegetables not specifically mentioned, allow 3–4 minutes per 450g (1lb).

When cooking foods frozen in a cooking bag, it is not necessary to drop them in boiling water. Just puncture the top of the bag to make a steam vent, place the bag on a plate to catch drips and microwave on HIGH the amount of time needed.

Drying Flowers and Herbs

The microwave oven enables you to dry flowers in a matter of minutes – which would take weeks conventionally! The quality is superior, the colours are brighter and the flowers are not as dry and perishable as conventionally dried ones.

NB Check that the manufacturer of your microwave recommends drying flowers and foliage in your oven.

Selecting flowers Flowers that dry especially well are roses, zinnias, asters, pansies, daisies, violets, carnations, daffodils, marigolds and chrysanthemums. Some flowers difficult to dry are tulips, irises and geraniums. Select flowers with bright colours; pick them just as they are reaching their peak of bloom. Avoid flowers with thick or densely clustered centres.

Drying agents:
Silica-gel, available in many craft shops, is the most satisfactory material. This is what we recommend using for the best quality dried flowers.

Borax/Cornmeal mixture, containing equal amounts of each can be used if Silica-gel is not available.

Sifted Cat Litter, made of ground clay, has a great deal of absorbing quality and can be used.

Each of these may be reused over and over.

Procedure:
Dry 3–4 flowers at a time. Select a microwave-safe container deep enough so the drying agent can cover the entire blooms. Pour the drying agent into a container to 1.25cm (½in) deep. Cut each flower stem to 1.25cm (½in) length. Place the flowers, head up, in the drying agent. With a spoon, gently sprinkle the agent around the outside of each flower until the bottom half is covered all around. Sprinkle the agent inside each flower and between the petals. Use a cocktail stick to separate the petals if needed. Place a cup of water in the corner of the oven to provide moisture in the

oven. Place the flowers, completely covered with drying agent, in the oven, uncovered, and microwave about 1–3 minutes.

Many variables affect drying time, such as the amount of moisture in the flowers and the size of the flowers. You can determine the appropriate drying time only by experiment.

Standing time is necessary for the flowers to cool off and set. After heating, let the flowers stand, undisturbed, in the drying agent for 1–2 hours to overnight. Some flowers give better results with a longer standing time. When the flowers are 'set', gently spoon away the drying agent to expose the flowers. Gently remove the flowers and lightly brush the flower petals with a soft artist's brush to remove particles of the drying agent.

A spray colouring agent may be applied to add more colour, if desired, but this is usually not needed since the colours of microwave-dried flowers are usually vivid. A colouring may be used months or years later to 'freshen' the arrangement, since the colours do tend to fade with time.

When flowers are dry, attach floral wires for stems. Make a hook in one end of the wire and pull it through the centre of the flower with the hook-end embedded in the centre. Use floral tape to secure the flower to the wire. A 'glue gun' is very handy for this if one is available. Just hold the stem wire against the flower stem and touch with the glue gun, instantly gluing the two together. Then use floral tape.

Drying without a drying agent: Leaves can be dried in the microwave without a drying agent, since they already have a low moisture content. Just place paper towels in the bottom of your oven, then layer leaves with paper towels to make several layers. Microwave on HIGH 1–1½ minutes, checking at 30 second intervals. If needed, turn the leaves and paper towels over and microwave 1–1½ minutes longer. Check the leaves to prevent over-drying. Magnolia branches and leaves, ferns and camelia foliage may be dried by this method also. Do not use recycled paper towels.

Herbs: Wash herb leaves to be dried and drain well. Place a few sprigs or a half-cupful between two paper towels and microwave on HIGH about 2 minutes or until dry. Check after 30 second intervals. Cool before storing in an air tight tin.

Bouquet Garni

Makes 1

2 cloves garlic, halved
1 bay leaf
4 sprigs parsley

2 × 5ml tsp (2tsp) snipped fresh
thyme or 3.75ml (¾tsp) dried
thyme

Cut a small square from several thicknesses of cheesecloth and place the ingredients in the centre. Bring corners of cheesecloth together to form a bag. Tie with string.

Pot-pourri

Pot-pourri is a mixture of dried flowers and leaves seasoned with spices and oils. It is kept in a covered jar to fill the room with fragrance when the lid is lifted.

1 litre (1¾pt) flower petals
25g (1oz) each: cinnamon,
    nutmeg, cloves and root ginger
15g (½oz) aniseed

50g (2oz) powdered arrowroot
Whole cloves
Crushed cinnamon sticks

Pot-pourri Garland

Gives off a subtle fragrance for many months. A delightful and unique way to display your 'microwave dried' flowers in any room of your house.

Materials needed:
Straw wreath base
Florist pins (U-shaped)
Spanish moss (optional)
Fresh herbs of your choice:
    rosemary, sage, thyme, fennel,
    lavender, etc (do not use rue! It
    has an overwhelming fragrance).

Dried flowers on wire stems
Other dried 'filler' materials:
    baby's breath, eucalyptus, citrus
    spirals, whole nutmeg on wire
    stems, etc.

Directions:
Take the green plastic wrapping off the straw wreath base. Mash or push the wreath into the desired shape. (We have made

triangular and oval wreaths.) Attach a small block of styrofoam with pins at the base. This will provide a place to attach a 'bouquet of flowers'. Wrap a wire around the top of the wreath to form a hanger.

Using florist pins, cover the wreath with Spanish moss. This step is not necessary if moss is unavailable, but it covers the straw and enables you to use less fresh herb sprigs.

Using florist pins, attach sprigs of fresh herbs to cover the wreath. Overlap the herbs so the pins do not show. They will dry naturally on the wreath.

Attach flowers and filler materials to form a floral spray. Spray lightly with clear acrylic spray to protect the flowers from humidity and to preserve the colours.

Herb Sachet

Mix equal amounts of rosemary, thyme and mint. Add some ground cloves. Tie in a little sachet bag.

Acknowledgements

Thanks to Joye H. Spates for her confidence and abiding faith in our abilities; Linda B. Wall for her inspiration and encouragement; our many friends for all their support; finally, special thanks to our parents.

Illustrations: Kay Loftis Lambert
Editorial consultant: Joe H. Wilkins Jr

Index

190